T0332894

Detection and Mitigation of Insider Attacks in a Cloud Infrastructure:

Emerging Research and Opportunities

T. Gunasekhar
Koneru Lakshmaiah Education Foundation, India

K. Thirupathi Rao
Koneru Lakshmaiah Education Foundation, India

P. Sai Kiran
Koneru Lakshmaiah Education Foundation, India

V. Krishna Reddy
Koneru Lakshmaiah Education Foundation, India

B. Thirumala Rao
Koneru Lakshmaiah Education Foundation, India

A volume in the Advances in
Information Security, Privacy, and
Ethics (AISPE) Book Series

Published in the United States of America by
  IGI Global
  Information Science Reference (an imprint of IGI Global)
  701 E. Chocolate Avenue
  Hershey PA, USA 17033
  Tel: 717-533-8845
  Fax: 717-533-8661
  E-mail: cust@igi-global.com
  Web site: http://www.igi-global.com

Library of Congress Cataloging-in-Publication Data

Names: Gunasekhar, T., 1990- author.
Title: Detection and mitigation of insider attacks in a cloud infrastructure
  : emerging research and opportunities / by T. Gunasekhar, K. Thirupathi
  Rao, P. Sai Kiran, V. Krishna Reddy, and B. Thirumala Rao.
Description: Hershey, PA : Information Science Reference, an imprint of IGI
  Global, [2019] | Includes bibliographical references.
Identifiers: LCCN 2018038726| ISBN 9781522579243 (hardcover) | ISBN
  9781522579250 (ebook)
Subjects: LCSH: Cloud computing--Security measures. | Virtual computer
  systems--Security measures. | Computer crimes--Prevention.
Classification: LCC QA76.585 .G86 2019 | DDC 004.67/82--dc23 LC record available at https://
lccn.loc.gov/2018038726

This book is published in the IGI Global book series Advances in Information Security, Privacy,
and Ethics (AISPE) (ISSN: 1948-9730; eISSN: 1948-9749)

British Cataloguing in Publication Data
A Cataloguing in Publication record for this book is available from the British Library.

All work contributed to this book is new, previously-unpublished material.
The views expressed in this book are those of the authors, but not necessarily of the publisher.

For electronic access to this publication, please contact: eresources@igi-global.com.

Advances in Information Security, Privacy, and Ethics (AISPE) Book Series

ISSN:1948-9730
EISSN:1948-9749

Editor-in-Chief: Manish Gupta, State University of New York, USA

MISSION

As digital technologies become more pervasive in everyday life and the Internet is utilized in ever increasing ways by both private and public entities, concern over digital threats becomes more prevalent.

The **Advances in Information Security, Privacy, & Ethics (AISPE) Book Series** provides cutting-edge research on the protection and misuse of information and technology across various industries and settings. Comprised of scholarly research on topics such as identity management, cryptography, system security, authentication, and data protection, this book series is ideal for reference by IT professionals, academicians, and upper-level students.

COVERAGE

- Device Fingerprinting
- Data Storage of Minors
- Information Security Standards
- IT Risk
- Global Privacy Concerns
- CIA Triad of Information Security
- Computer ethics
- Electronic Mail Security
- Cyberethics
- Access Control

IGI Global is currently accepting manuscripts for publication within this series. To submit a proposal for a volume in this series, please contact our Acquisition Editors at Acquisitions@igi-global.com or visit: http://www.igi-global.com/publish/.

Titles in this Series

For a list of additional titles in this series, please visit:
https://www.igi-global.com/book-series/advances-information-security-privacy-ethics/37157

Advanced Methodologies and Technologies in System Security, Information Privacy, ...
Mehdi Khosrow-Pour, D.B.A. (Information Resources Management Association, USA)
Information Science Reference • ©2019 • 417pp • H/C (ISBN: 9781522574927) • US $285.00

Handbook of Research on Information and Cyber Security in the Fourth Industrial Revolution
Ziska Fields (University of KwaZulu-Natal, South Africa)
Information Science Reference • ©2018 • 647pp • H/C (ISBN: 9781522547631) • US $345.00

Security and Privacy in Smart Sensor Networks
Yassine Maleh (University Hassan I, Morocco) Abdellah Ezzati (University Hassan I, Morocco) and Mustapha Belaissaoui (University Hassan I, Morocco)
Information Science Reference • ©2018 • 441pp • H/C (ISBN: 9781522557364) • US $215.00

The Changing Scope of Technoethics in Contemporary Society
Rocci Luppicini (University of Ottawa, Canada)
Information Science Reference • ©2018 • 403pp • H/C (ISBN: 9781522550945) • US $225.00

Handbook of Research on Information Security in Biomedical Signal Processing
Chittaranjan Pradhan (KIIT University, India) Himansu Das (KIIT University, India) Bighnaraj Naik (Veer Surendra Sai University of Technology (VSSUT), India) and Nilanjan Dey (Techno India College of Technology, India)
Information Science Reference • ©2018 • 414pp • H/C (ISBN: 9781522551522) • US $325.00

Handbook of Research on Network Forensics and Analysis Techniques
Gulshan Shrivastava (National Institute of Technology Patna, India) Prabhat Kumar (National Institute of Technology Patna, India) B. B. Gupta (National Institute of Technology Kurukshetra, India) Suman Bala (Orange Labs, France) and Nilanjan Dey (Techno India College of Technology, India)
Information Science Reference • ©2018 • 509pp • H/C (ISBN: 9781522541004) • US $335.00

For an entire list of titles in this series, please visit:
https://www.igi-global.com/book-series/advances-information-security-privacy-ethics/37157

701 East Chocolate Avenue, Hershey, PA 17033, USA
Tel: 717-533-8845 x100 • Fax: 717-533-8661
E-Mail: cust@igi-global.com • www.igi-global.com

Table of Contents

Preface

Cloud Computing is an emerging and promising paradigm that allows cloud clients to store their data and computing resources on demand with pay-per-usage model. An additional feature of a cloud computing makes flourish and more successful than the Grid computing such as auto-scaling, low cost and multi tenancy. A wide adoption of cloud services leads to an insider attack, which greatly damages the data confidentiality and integrity in cloud environment. Cloud provider can ensure data integrity and confidentiality by constantly storing cloud user data in encrypted format and decrypt those on the cloud platform. This approach leads to high computational cost and it is not practical in cloud platforms. The homomorphic encryption schemes, performs computations on encrypted data then generates result as an outsourced. The decryption operation matches result of operations performed on original data. These methods generates large amount of overheads in performing operation and in practical only primitive operations are supported in cloud environment. Any operation performed in IaaS cloud should be transparent to cloud client, it is a strong requirement in cloud infrastructure.

Detection and Mitigation of Insider Attacks in a Cloud Infrastructure: Emerging Research and Opportunities is organized into six chapters. The introduction introduces the basics of cloud computing, virtualization, insider attacks, insider attacks in cloud computing, and Trusted computing. This chapter gives the clear problem that we targeted in the whole book. At the end of this chapter we have given some research directions to solve the addressed problem.

Chapter 1 provides the brief information about security architecture of cloud environment. The security architecture gives the security flaws in virtualization, cloud storage integrity and privacy, and infrastructure level security issues. At the end of this chapter, research directions provides set of solutions to solve the targeted issues.

Chapter 2 provides the information about trusted computing and trusted cloud computing. This chapter elaborates the Trusted Platform Module along with trustworthy computing in traditional computing environments. This allows a reader to explore the various protocols which are used to validate and verify the given cloud resources.

Chapter 3 provides a literature survey about the addressed problems in the cloud infrastructure. The literature is categorized into five approaches: First, cryptographic approaches provides various encryption and decryption scheme to secure the consumer virtual machine in the cloud computing. Second, trusted computing based approaches uses the remote attestation and integrity measurement to provide the solution for the insider attacks. Third, Encryption based approaches deals with the consumer virtual machine encryption standards to ensure the virtual machine integrity. Fourth, virtualization based approaches deals with virtual machine along virtual trusted computing frameworks, such as vTPM, TrustVisor, etc. Fifth, public key cryptography provides an information about public key based approaches to mitigate the insider attacks on cloud resources.

Chapter 4 elaborates an empirical approaches to exhibits security vulnerability in the virtualization. This attacks vector is performed in multiple location of cloud infrastructure to address the flaws present in the current virtualization schemes.

Chapter 5 provides an information about the proposed framework to detect and mitigate the insider attacks in cloud through trusted cloud computing protocols. In this framework, the remote attestation and integrity measurement (IMA) plays a major role to achieve the virtual machine integrity and confidentiality. proposed a protocol that ensures integrity and confidentiality of client computations and data in cloud infrastructure. Cloud provider has to ensure that private is not exposed to external entities as well as internal entities such as cloud clients and cloud administrators. Our protocol uses the sealed storage, performs encryption on specified memory location using Storage Root Key (SRK). It ensures confidentiality of memory resources of VM. Remote attestation, trusted third party verifies platform integrity and TrustVisor (McCune, 2010), provides an isolated execution environment for VM to ensure integrity and computation confidentiality. We have implemented the protocol by extending our concept with open source cloud called Eucalyptus (Nurmi, 2009). TCB is minimized when compared to the Flicker (McCune,2008), and it takes less overhead while performing TPM operations.

Chapter 6 provides the performance evaluation of proposed framework with remote attestation, trusted computing base, trusted platform module execution and boot process. The evaluated results shows the better performance when compared with various approaches. (Those are presented in Chapter 3.) The conclusion gives the summary of the complete proposed scheme and future work.

I wanted to take this opportunity to welcome you to your education on Cloud security. Writing this book has been a lot of fun for me and I sincerely hope that you get a lot out of it. I have tried to be balanced in presenting both the advantages and disadvantages of some of the new ideas. I encourage you to adopt a similar open and critical stance when reading this book.

Tell all your friends about this book. I hope to make it accessible to the widest possible audience and I need your help in achieving this objective.

Introduction

This introduction provides the insider threat definition followed by the basics of cloud computing, virtualization, Trustworthy computing, research directions and thesis organization. Cloud Computing is an emerging and promising technology that allows cloud clients to store their data and rent computing resources on demand with pay-per-usage model. An additional feature such as auto-scaling, low cost and multi tenancy in cloud computing makes more successful than the Grid computing. A wide adoption of cloud services leads to an insider attack, which greatly damages the data confidentiality and integrity in cloud environment.

According to the computer emergency response team (CERT) definition of insider threat "A malicious insider threat to an organization is a current or former employee, contractor, or other business partner who has or had authorized access to an organization's network, system, or data and intentionally exceeded or misused that access in a manner that negatively affected the confidentiality, integrity, or availability of the organization's information or information systems"(Cappelli, D. M et.al., 2012). The damages of insider threat are: IT sabotages, theft of confidential information, trade secrets and Intellectual property (IP). 85% of reported fraud is committed by people within the organization. A typical organization loose approximately 5% of its annual revenue due to insider fraud and 330 cases of insider fraud identified during 2010. Therefore, it is important for every organization to maintain a secure management of sensitive data and intellectual property. In cloud environment, most of the insider threat can be done by cloud insiders such that cloud service provider should provide robust security algorithm on consumer data. This work provides a prototype for securing data at data centers as well as at organizational databases. According to the Internet threat resource center, 24% of data breaches that reported from financial institutions during 2008 and twenty percent of government information breaches and, sixteen percent of private business data breaches were caused by insider attacks. 50 percent of government websites vulnerable, those have no security mechanisms.

INSIDER THREAT DEFINITION

The easiest way to get the definition of Insider threat by dividing two words each other. According to dictionary.cambridge.org, an insider can be defined as "someone who is an accepted member of a group and who therefore has special or secret knowledge or influence and Threat as a suggestion that something unpleasant or violent will happen, especially if a particular action or order is not followed". Putting this definition together, an insider threat can be anyone who has legitimate access to the organization with a malicious intent. The insider threats are so powerful and major companies not aware of it.

Unauthorized vs. Authorized Insiders

An insider is anyone who has privileged access to company database and insider attack is made by those peoples with their access credentials to destroy or modify/copy the data centers. In most company's problems are occurred through giving most privileges to the insiders and they can steal the sensitive information at a high level of intensity. The risks of insider threats are with the employees with auxiliary privileges, which it leads to huge damage. If the cloud service providers give the access rights to minimum number of peoples who are working for the same organization, the possibility of insider threat problem could be minimized. It is easy to monitor minimum people instead of huge one and threats could be easy to detect and correct. Therefore, the vast insiders with access privileges to access the sensitive information, leads to lose of data confidentiality and integrity of the cloud consumers in the cloud infrastructure(Cappelli, D. M et.al., 2012)..

Cloud Computing

Cloud computing relates to the delivery of cloud services on internet, by keeping your own private information in hard disk, pc or updating the applications for your needs, you use services among Internet. In these applications, the data will store in another location. It may rise to privacy issues. When you hide, or store your data online instead of on your pc or Google drive or mail, you are using cloud computing services. This cloud model allows the information to access from anywhere with an internet or network connection is available. According to NIST definition has been developed "Cloud computing is a model for enabling convenient, on-demand network access to shared pool of configurable computing resources that can be rapidly provisioned and released with minimal management effort or service provider interaction". The below Figure 1 describes brief definition about the NIST architecture (Mell, P., & Grance, T. 2011).

Figure 1. NIST Cloud computing architecture

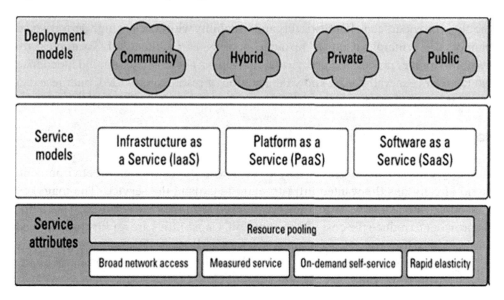

This cloud has five characteristics, three service models, and four deployment models. The characteristics are on-demand self-service, broad network access, Response pooling, rapid elasticity, and measured service.

On Demand Self-Service

In cloud computing, network services such as e-mail, network, applications or server services be provided without need of humans with service provider interaction. Cloud service providers providing on demand self-services include Salesforce. com, Amazon Web Services (AWS), Microsoft, IBM and Google. Consumer can able to provide cloud resources, and no need of requiring human interaction with every server provider.

Broad Network Access

In this, the network of cloud can access from anywhere and access by any device such as laptop, smart phones, etc. instead of user to be in a particular location. By the help of recent wireless services, users can have good quality of services from anywhere they go. In reference of cloud, user can access cloud service with wireless device to use IP network which is convenient.

Resource Pooling

The cloud providers can offer flexibility and scalability with efficient high performance manner, the principle using is resource pooling as architectural. Examples are memory storage, processing and virtual machines. There is location independence that the users generally don't know the location of resource provided, but these can access through intranet.

Rapid Scalable and Elasticity

Elasticity can be able to grow easily to deal with demand in cloud environment. Cloud already has the wanted infrastructure to expand the service. The main key is resources are available even; they are no used until they are required. This helps the provider to reduce the cost of consumption. Capabilities are rapidly provisioned automatically in some cases for quick sale out and released rapidly for quick sale in. The resources for provisioning offer to be unlimited and it can purchase at any quantity within any time.

Measured Service

Cloud administrations must be able to measure usage. The usage can be examined using metrics like bandwidth, time, and data used. This service enables pay as you go feature of cloud. Once correct metrics identified then the rate is defined. This rate depends on customer charged, like this client bills based on usage level. If anybody is paying for services of cloud they need to know about which services are measured and which service are charged. In this measured service, it is very important to know about the appropriate cost.

SERVICE MODELS

With reference of service oriented architecture, cloud's modular and reusable approach many services are provided by it. The word XaaS has to mean anything as a Service. We are in world where anyone can access internet. Clients have been demanding data and applications conveyed through web. This is going about as an impetus to the ascent of XaaS. An expanding number of services are being offered through cloud or web. The most widely recognized administrations from XaaS categories.

The NIST definition of cloud computing explained about three service models they are Infrastructure as a service (IaaS), Platform as a service (PaaS), Software as a service (SaaS), here we will cover these models briefly.

1. **Infrastructure as a Service:** IaaS gives virtual machines, virtual capacity, virtual framework, and other equipment assets as asset that customers can procurement. IaaS administration supplier deals with the entire framework, while the customer is in charge of every single other part of the organization. This can incorporate the working framework, applications and client associations with the framework.

2. **Platform as a Service:** PaaS gives virtual machines, working frameworks, applications, administrations, improvement systems, exchanges, and control structures. The customer can send its applications on the cloud base or utilization applications that were modified utilizing devices that are supported by the PaaS administration supplier. The administration supplier deals with the cloud infrastructure, the working frameworks, and the enabling software. The customer is in charge of introducing and dealing with the application that is sending.

3. **Software as a Service:** SaaS is a complete working environment with applications, administration, and client interface. In the SaaS model, the application is given to the customer through a customer interface, and the client's obligation starts and finishes with entering and dealing with its information and client cooperation. Everything starting from the application to the foundation is the seller's obligation.

Cloud Deployment Models

The way cloud is utilized from association to association. Each association has its own prerequisites in the matter of what administrations it needs to access from cloud and the amount of control it needs to have over environment. To oblige these changing prerequisites, a cloud domain can be executed utilizing distinctive administration models. Each administration model has its own arrangement of necessities and advantages. The NIST definition of cloud computing has four cloud deployment models: public, private, community, and hybrid.

Public Cloud

Public cloud allows systems and services to be easily accessible to public. Public cloud may be less secure because of its openness. In general society administration had shown every one of the frameworks and resources that give the administration are housed at an outside administration supplier. That administration supplier is in charge of the administration and administration of the frameworks that are utilized to give the administration. The customer is in charge of any product or customer application that is introduced on the end client framework. Associations with open cloud suppliers are normally made through the web.

Private Cloud

In a private cloud, the frameworks and assets that give the administration are found inside to organization or association that uses them. That association is in charge of the administration and organization of the frameworks that are utilized to give administration. Moreover, the association is likely in charge of any product or customer application that is introduced on the end-client framework. Private clouds are generally acquired through the neighborhood LAN or Wide Area Network (WAN). On account of remote clients, In general resource access will be provided through Internet or through virtual private network (VPN).

Community Cloud

Group clouds are semi-open clouds that are shared between individuals from a select gathering of organizations. These associations will for the most part have a typical reason or mission. The associations would prefer not to utilize an open cloud that is interested in each one. They need more security than what an open cloud offers. In expansion, every association wouldn't like to be separately in charge of keeping up the cloud; they need to have the capacity to impart the obligations to others.

Hybrid Cloud

Hybrid cloud model is a blend of two or more other cloud models. The clouds themselves are not combined; rather, every cloud is separate, and they are all connected. A hybrid cloud may acquaint more many-sided quality with nature, yet it additionally permits more adaptability in satisfying an organizations destination.

Major Components of Cloud Computing

According to NIST It is a generic high level language computational model that is an intense instrument for examining the necessities, structures and operations of distributed computing. The model is not fixing to any merchant, items, administrations, or reference execution, nor does it characterize point of view arrangements that possess development(Mell, P., & Grance, T. 2011)..

It characterizes set of actors, functions and activities that can be utilized as a part of the procedure of sending distributed computing architectures, and identifies with a companion distributed computing scientific categorization. It has five main roles and responsibilities with a companion distributed computing scientific categorization. It has five major actors: Cloud consumer, Cloud provider, Cloud auditor, Cloud broker and Cloud carrier

1. **Cloud Consumer:** A person or association that keeps up a business association with clients and administrations from cloud suppliers.
2. **Cloud Provider:** A person, or association, or entity responsible of making an administration accessible to invested individuals.
3. **Cloud Auditor:** A party that can conduct independent assessment of cloud administrations, data framework operations, execution and security of the cloud usage.
4. **Cloud Broker:** An entity that deals with the utilization, execution and delivery of cloud administrations, and arranges connections between cloud providers and cloud customers.
5. **Cloud Carrier:** It acts like a bridge between cloud service provider and cloud consumer to transport of cloud services through internet connectivity

CLOUD COMPUTING SECURITY ISSUES

Security is for the most part seen as a large issue of the cloud. The review observed that while 58% of all general community and 86% of senior business pioneers are exited up for the capability of cloud computing more than 90% of these same individuals are joined about the security access and protect their own information in the cloud. There is probability where a malicious client cans penetrate the cloud by impersonating an appropriate client, there by tainting the whole cloud along these lines influencing numerous clients who are sharing the contaminated cloud. Some of the security problems which are faced by the cloud computing are: Data integrity, data theft, security on vendor level, security on user level and Information security.

Data Integrity and Theft

At the point when information is on a cloud anybody from any area can get to that information's from cloud. Cloud doesn't individuate between delicate information from typical information thus allow anybody to get to those delicate data's. Hence there is an absence of information trustworthiness in cloud computing (Romanosky, S., et.al,. 2011).

Most of the cloud sellers rather than gaining a server tries to let a server from other administration providers of the fact that they are expensive and adaptable for operation. The client doesn't think about the things there is a high probability that the information can be stolen from the outside server by malicious client. Merchant verified that server is all around secured from external outside threat it may run over. A cloud is great only if there is a good security gave by the seller to the client. Even merchant provided quality security layer to client, the client ought to verify due to its own particular activity, there shouldn't be any losing of information tampering of information for others clients who are present in the same cloud.

Information Security

The security identified with data exchanged between various hosts or in the middle of hosts and clients. This issue relating to secure validation, communication, authentication and issues concerns with single sign on and designation.

Concerns in this category include the following:

1. Physical security
2. Operational security.

Physical Security and Data Location

Physical area of server centers; assurance of server data against disaster and instruction. How to save the data from Natural disaster? Information can be needlessly store in different physical area. Physical area ought to be distributed over world. In general, cloud clients don't know the definite area of the datacenter furthermore they don't have any control over the physical access instruments to that information. Most known cloud administration suppliers have data centers around the world. In many a cases, this may be an issue. Because of compliance and information security laws in different countries, locality of information is of most extreme importance in much enterprise architecture.

To maintain data security in distributed system, transactions over multiple information sources should handle safely in fail safe manner. This should be done by central world-wide transaction manager. Every application in the distributed system can able to take part in world-wide transaction by means of resource manager. When client utilize the cloud, client probably won't know exactly where your information is facilitated, in which country it will be stored in.

Traditional Security

These security issues include PC and network intrusions or attacks that make possible or at least simplest by moving to the cloud. Cloud providers react to these involves by arguing that the measures in security and procedures are more develop and tried than those of the normal organization. Another argument, made by the Jericho Forum (Don't Cloud Vision) is: "It could be easier to lock down information if it's administered by a third party rather than in-house, if companies are worried about insider threats. In addition, it may be easier to enforce security via contracts with online services providers than via internal controls".

VM-Level Attacks

Potential vulnerabilities in the VM technology utilized by cloud sellers are a potential issue in multi-tenant architectures. Vulnerabilities have appeared in VMware (Security Tracker: VMware Shared Folder Bug), Xen (Xen Vulnerability), and Microsoft's Virtual PC and Virtual Server. Vendors such as Third Brigade mitigate potential VM-level vulnerabilities through monitoring and firewalls (Kim, T., et.al,.2012).

Denial of Service Attacks in Cloud

Cloud computing is rapid growing in IT business innovations. Most of the IT companies announce strategies for products to cloud environment. Cloud computing is presently one of the growing IT innovations. Most of the IT companies announced to plan products according to the cloud computing paradigm. Because of the cloud simplicity itself not matured yet, already proven that most of the critical threats as per public concerns in security. In the future, we can expect more security concern events to cloud service provider and clients; those will help us to new security research directions in the cloud environment. We have seen a rapid evolution of cloud computing security environment, which will effects on ongoing requirements and security and privacy issues raises. Because of these issues and concerns the cloud computing authors monitoring security attacks over a network and hacking is made by cloud components to gain the controls of those. The security vulnerabilities and security concerns should take specification to address the issues accordingly.

In this section, we provide variety of attacks over a network based cloud components in the cloud environment and we give taxonomy of DOS attacks based on the notion of attack nature.

CLOUD COMPUTING ATTACKS

Due to cloud simplicity, companies migrating to cloud computing environment. The following are some of the potential attacks, which might be attempt by insiders or outsiders.

1. Denial of Service (DOS)attacks
2. Cloud Malware Injection Attack
3. Side Channel Attacks
4. Authentication Attacks
5. Man-In-The-Middle Attacks

Denial of Service (DOS) Attacks

The denial of service attacks mainly focus on web resources, those are provided by cloud service provider. Some of the security professionals suggested that cloud is vulnerable to denial of service attacks, because of its sharing of resources among their clients. The DOS attacks ensure more damage to the compromised resources in cloud environment. The cloud computing operating system poses the heavy workloads on distributed services, then the cloud try to provide more computing power to the resources about workloads. Thus, the server component boundaries are extended to maximum workload to process for no longer hold. By this way the cloud host is try to work against intruder up to some extent even it supports the attackers by damaging services on resources. Due to this activity service availability decreased. The Figure 2 shows a model of DOS attack done by intruder. Thus, the intruder no need flood to all n resources in target, but instead it can flood as single. The cloud-based environment address in order to perform a huge loss of availability on specific services. A cloud service provider cannot able to share secured data among its clients that address to the difficulty of in identification by cloud clients. A Denial of Service (DOS) attack is an attack that compromise a website, causing the resources normally issued by the website those no longer for clients of that website. Distributed Denial of Service (DDOS) attacks are based on traffic volume-based attacks from huge number of compromised hosts. These hosts or resources, known as 'zombies', form a widely distributed attack network called as 'botnet'. The resource attacks in cloud are distributed denial of service; this may not be true for denial of services in the websites. Therefore, when user experiencing difficulty to access websites content, it should not be assumed ad denial service attack (Yan, Q., & Yu, F. R. 2015).

Many forms of DOS attacks are easier implement than DDOS attacks and these attacks are still used by intruders with malicious intent. The DOS attacks are easier to defend using mechanisms which are known to the cloud client. It is important to complete analysis of attacks when website becomes perform unusual functions. Such that, it is essential to analysis of attack traffic when a website becomes unable to perform its usual role. Most of the DOS attack mechanisms are super finely enforced at good at that time. Some mechanisms, those are varieties types of website resemble

Figure 2. DOS attack in cloud-computing

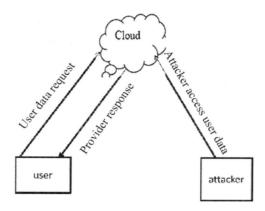

are enforced as general operating procedure to check whether the website is attacked or not. These methods are models for our website, those are good for performance and resilience to DOS attacks. Other mechanisms are organized to reactivate the websites, those are under DOS attacks.

Types of DOS Attacks

DOS attacks are broadly classified based on Network based and attacker's behavior. The network-based DOS attacks are:

1. UDP Bombing
2. TCP SYN Flooding
3. Ping of Death
4. Smurf Attack

These attacks are possibly on the network resources and are explained. The network-based attacks play an important role in cloud environment.

UDP Bombing Attack

The UDP bombing attack is a network-based attack. In this we reckoned two UDP services: echo and chargen, these are used in the early network monitoring and testing and, are enabled as default on most systems. These two UDP services can be used to launch DOS attack by connecting the chargen to echo ports on the similar or another hosts and produces huge amount of network traffic.

UDP Service Denial

Chargen and Disable echo are countermeasures of UDP denial of services and remaining services are unused such as/etc/inetd. Config in UNIX operating system, and Cisco ensures UDP with no small services at the firewall level. It only allows legitimate traffic such on UDP port 53 by monitoring on firewalls.

Windows UDP Attacks

The Microsoft windows operating systems are vulnerable to UDP attacks than in the UNIX operating system. The tools those exploits the weakness of windows operating systems are Bonk, Boink, and Newt ear bonk. The possible weakness exploits in windows 9.x/IP stack/NT TCP. The hacker can send malformed packets to the vulnerable host in a network and packets are re-assembled as invalid UDP datagram. By receiving the invalid packets, the host reboots or freezes with blank screens. This effect is also called as pathological offset attack.

TCP SYN Flooding

TCP SYN flooding is also referred to as the TCP half open attack in order to establish a authorized TCP connection then the user sends a SYN packet from host to the server.

1. The client sends a SYN
2. ACK back to the client
3. The client sends an ACK back to the server

Here, the three-way handshaking connection is established, and attack did by the attacker through the initialization of a TCP connection to the server. The connection can be established with the usage SYN and legitimate source address. The server sends ACK as response to clients SYN packet then server wait for clients reply and allocates memory for that client. This leads to wastage of memory and server time.

TCP SYN Flooding

The connection established under the three ways handshaking will suffers from DOS attacks. After establishment of half open connection, the victim server will buffer connection request until reply from client. No connection will be made till the buffer becomes emptied. There is timeout policy in such case of half connections, so that connection will be terminated after time expires. The attacker continuously sends connection request with SYN packet faster than the server expires the pending connection requests. To overcome these types of network-based attacks, there are different countermeasures those are explained below clearly (Darwish, M., Ouda, A., et.al,.2013).

TCP SYN Flooding: Countermeasures

There are different countermeasures for the TCP SYN flooding attacks in the network-based topologies

1. Claim vendor patches on newly released Operating systems to optimize the problems.
2. Install filters on routes to prevent IP spoofing in a network.

Ping of Death Attack

The ping of death is a denial of service attack caused by the attacker. The attacker can send an IP packet more than 65,536 bytes, which is allowable by the IP protocol. This is one of the features of TCP/IP protocol by fragmenting incoming packets into sub packets. The IP protocol allows a single packet and broken down into smaller packets. From 1996, the attackers took advantage of this feature when they found the packet broken in to small packet those could be add up to more than 65,536 bytes. Many operating systems don't know what has to do whenever it receives an extra sized packet. Such that the operating systems simply froze, rebooted and/or crashed. For clear clarification see Fig 1.2. Ping of death attacks were specifically dreadful because the identity of the intruder sending an extra sized packet can results in spoofing of packets and because the attacker no need to aware of machine details except the IP address of that machine in internet. To avoid these type attacks, the operating system companies released patches but still so many of websites under the blocking of Internet Control Message Protocol (ICMP) messages. These messages are filtered at firewall to prevent ping of death attacks and any features that related kind of denial service attacks.

Smurf Attack

The smurf attack is a kind of denial of service attack by exploiting on the internet protocol. It broadcast the addresses to create a denial of service attacks. The intruder uses the features of smurf program to cause that network to be inoperable. The smurf attack takes certain advantages over an Internet protocol (IP) and ICMP by using characteristics of these protocols over an internet. The ICMP is used by network components and administrators among nodes to exchange.

The ICMP can be used to send error notification messages among the nodes to the server. The operational node returns reply with an echo message in response to the message of ping. The smurf program generates an internet packet that seems to sends from other address for clear understand see Figure 3 and 4 IP packet contains ICMP ping notification and the entire network resources address in given network.

The ping messages are sent as echo to reply back to the vulnerable address. These ping and echo messages can flood the network traffic which is unusable network traffic. The possible overwhelming of these smurf attacks is to by not using IP address at each network router or resources.

Figure 3. Ping of death attack

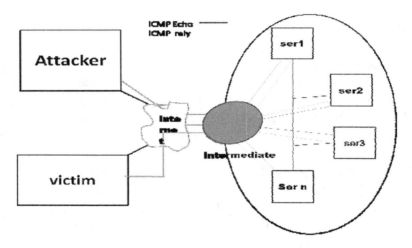

Figure 4. Smurf attack

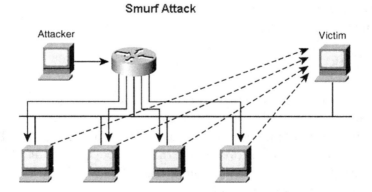

These attacks are happen over a network in cloud environment. The cloud computing mainly suffers from these attacks because it is operated based on network components. The cloud computing environment is network based services and cloud components are only access by network .

VIRTUALIZATION

Virtualization plays a major role in cloud computing paradigm, especially in Infrastructure as a Service model. This subsection provides detailed information about the virtualization basics, security flaws in present virtualization system and finally some security mechanisms of the virtualization techniques.

The extended machine concept limitations are reduced by introducing the virtualization technique(Goldberg, R. P., 1974). This architecture was developed in 70's third generation architectures and multi-programming OS/360 (Denning, P. J., 1971). Generally, a set of non-privileged instructions along with hyper calls or system call are included in the extended machine, without access of any authorized instruction execution. This states that without access privileges, it is not possible to replicate the base metal hypervisor machine. The major limitation of this architecture is that it does not support multi operating system on one physical machine (Goldberg, R. P., 1974).

The major components of the virtualization systems are: *Virtual Machines (VMs)* and *Virtual Machine Monitor (VMM)*. The virtual machine is not a physical machine, which is simulated on physical operating systems with necessary techniques. An extended machine approach was overcome with the innovations in the virtual systems.

The virtual machine monitor provides a facility to transform the single machine operation to many. This states that very virtual machines on the physical operating system is replica, which is running in logical manner with every instruction set of the host machine along with required host machine resources.

The virtualization architecture illustrated in Figure 5, which is introduced by IBM in 70s (Goldberg, R. P., 1974).. As the figure shows that every virtual machine has its own guest operating system, then the applications are executed on top of the guest operating system. As per the definitions from the IBM, the term full virtualization is utilized to reference the illustrated architecture in the Figure 5.

The virtual machine monitor also called as hypervisor, which monitors or manages the virtual machines on physical machine. The full virtualization is also referred as bare metal or native virtualization because the hypervisor can make a direct communication with bare metal physical virtual machine monitor, which controls the flow of instruction between the physical machine hardware and virtual machines (Scarfone, K. A., et.al,. 2011).. This thesis mainly focuses on the virtualization of

Figure 5. Native virtualization

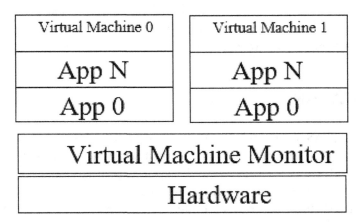

consumer data with privacy and confidentiality in x86 architecture. This virtualization platform initiated with VMware back in 90s (VMWare, 2007). In general, three x86 platform are full virtualization through binary translation, Para virtualization, and hardware assisted virtualization. Brief information about each technique follows.

Full Virtualization: Binary Translation

Full virtualization through binary translation x86 platform was major virtualization technique invented by VMware in 1998 (VMWare, 2007). The VMware solved the problem of ritualizing the critical x86 instruction, that major research organizations believed that it is impossible. Which is solved by concatenate the direct execution and binary translation of the instruction.

The direct execution with binary translation of x86 instructions of user applications, such as unprivileged application level instructions. The guest operating system or virtual machine contains non-virtualized x86 instructions. The binary translation can be assured by replacing the non-virtualizable x86 instructions with suitable new instructions, which are understandable by the virtual machine monitor or hypervisor. Using those instructions virtual machine monitor generates the desired request to designated virtual hardware. The binary translation provides the permission to execute the non-privileged instructions of user applications on top of the physical hardware to assure the high throughput performance.

The direct execution and binary translation guarantees full virtualization for the guest operating system executing as a virtual machine on top of the physical machine with non-privileged instruction set. This clearly states that, any operating system doesn't need any updation and it is completely unaware that is executing under the control and on top of the virtualization layer, which contains the VMM for each virtual machine to provide the complete virtualization services to the launched virtual machine. The virtual machine monitors or hypervisors are responsible for providing the physical machine resources to the expected such as virtual devices, virtual machine memory management and a virtual Basic input/output System (BIOS).

Para Virtualization

Para virtualization is another virtualization technique to handle the non-privileged and non-virtualizable x86 instruction set. The Para virtualization method mainly relies on the design of operating system and virtual machine monitor or hypervisor (Whitaker, A., et.al., 2002).

The operating system level instructions are executed from the Para virtualization by generating hypercalls while user application usually to perform the non-privileged instruction set to ensure the high performance. Hypercalls are same as traditional system calls of the user application use in non-virtualized environments to request the system kernel. In an hypercall, however, it is the operating system requesting a privileged operation to the *virtual machine monitor*.

An advantage of Para virtualization improves the scalability, simplicity, and performance (Whitaker, A., et.al., 2002). A major advantage of Para virtualization, it doesn't require hardware- assisted virtualization, but virtualization has some disadvantages. For instance, a guest operating system can only execute in a Para virtualized environment if its kernel is modified so it uses hyper calls to interact with the virtual machine monitor. These changes increase maintenance costs and prevent off the shelf operating systems from executing in para virtualized platforms.

Hardware-Assisted Virtualization

Para Virtualization and binary translation are imagined to overcome the problem of non-virtualized instruction of the x86 architecture requirements. Generally, x86 architecture provides four levels of access privileges to the user such as rings 0, 1, 2, and 3. When operating system moving away from the ring 0 so the VMM can take it as software with most access privilege levels. A single operating system with designed architecture, if the change happens the authorized operating system instructions are doesn't executed as it designed as well as it is not in ring 0 privileges. When the architecture redesigns the designer should consider the virtualization requirement that should be improve to implement the architecture as per the new design of operating system architecture.

Hardware-assisted virtualization is a better design to accommodate the requirements of the virtual machine systems. In the hardware assisted virtualization architecture, the hardware support provides the new root privilege level i.e., root level, where virtual machine hypervisor or virtual machine monitor execute the instructions at highest level than the ring 0 privileges. Suppose the virtual machine monitor present in the architecture, operating system privileged x86 instructions are set to automatically transfer platform control the hypervisor or virtual machine monitor. This procedure removes the burden of continues para virtualization in binary translation.

The hardware-assisted virtualization is implemented in major computer vendors such as AMD's virtualization technology (AMD-V) and Intel's virtualization technology (Intel VT) (Intel, 2014). The various features in the hardware assisted virtualization takes fast control transfer to the virtual machine monitor from the guest operating system and it has an ability to assign the physical input/output to the designated operating system. This provides the greater execution ability without taking the translation of x86 instruction execution and throughput of the system can assured through the execution time that elapsed from the initiation of execution.

TRUSTWORTHY COMPUTING

Trusted Platform Module is an international security standard for crypto- processors, which is a microprocessor developed to secure both firmware and software by integrating cryptographic keys in the tampered device. Major computer vendors such as Intel, Dell, HP and IBM (Trusted Computing Group, 2014a) have written a TPM's technical consortium called "Trusted Computing Group" and an International Organization for Standardization (ISO) and International Electro Technical Commission standardized the technical consortium of TPM as ISO/IEC 11889 in 2009. The main intension of TCG is to provide a trust in devices such as PC, PDAs and mobile devices and to provide transparent view to user about their platform. TPM provides a secure method for storing cryptographic keys, passwords and certificates used for personal usage, which is safe method for storing them in hardware instead hard disk.

TPM consists of finite set of Platform Configuration Registers(PCRs) that allows secure storage and cryptographic relevant metrics for reporting about integrity while attestation of platform (Greene,J., 2010), (Strongin, G., 2005). The PCR values are provided to external trusted parties using remote attestation to verify the trustworthiness of designated platform. The Trusted Computing Base(TCB) of a system is a finite set of software, hardware and/or software components that are essential for security of intact system. The external components of system i.e., outside TCB should not breach security policies and should not get any privileges than granted privileges. Vulnerabilities within TCB affect or compromises security of the entire system.

Trusted Platform Module

The Trusted Platform Module (TPM) is defined by Trusted Computing Group, which is crypto processor with capacity of storing digital certificates, keys and passwords (Trusted Computing Group, 2014b). The TPM provides the secure storage as well as tamper-protected environment as tamper evident and resistance. This property disallows the physical tampering of TPM module and related components (Trusted Computing Group, 2007b).

A TPM has set feature among those a root *of trust* is a software or hardware mechanism to allow the authorized user to implicitly trust. The tamper-resistance and evident feature make is as logic for the root of trust. In general, the root of trust has three roots of trusts, such as root for trust for storage(RTS), root for trust for reporting(RTR) and root for measurement (RTM) (Trusted Computing Group, 2007b). The trusted Platform Module is shown in Figure 6.

1. **Root of Trust for Measurement (RTM):** This TPM feature ensure the reliable implementation of a hash function, those are may or may not be within the tamper- resistant TPM module. Before suing this hash function, it be trust and it should be able to provide the integrity measurement in establishing the trustworthiness of the platform. The RTM collect and store cryptographic hash functions to establish the trustworthiness of the software components or data with the designated measurements.
2. **Root of Trust for Storage (RTS):** The TPM must provide the secure storage of software or data which is resided in the system premises. The TPM integrity measurement should be store in tamper evident and resistance.

Figure 6. Rusted Platform Modules (TPM).

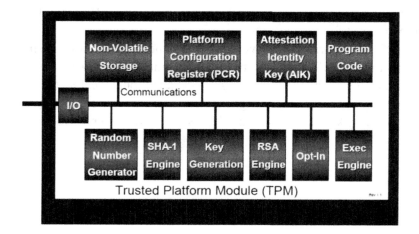

3. **Root of Trust for Reporting (RTR):** The integrity measurements of TPM components and mechanisms involved in reporting must be verifiable to check the integrity of the system components.

These roots of trust mechanisms provide the integrity or trustworthiness of the TPM-enabled system platforms and these are building blocks of the trustworthiness of the target platform. The Figure 6 shows major components of the TPM module according to the Trusted Computing Group(TCG) standards. The related topics and major building blocks are introduced together with the functionality they enable in the TCG standards and which are discussed in the following subsections

Cryptographic Keys and Data Storage

The Trusted Platform Module contains both volatile and non-volatile data storage. The non-volatile storage is important when storing the storage root key, endorsement key (EK), and related data to manage the TPM modules. Because of its security delicate nature, these keys are put away in protected areas just available through an arrangement of orders with the required permissions (Trusted Computing Group, 2007b) & (Grawrock, D., 2009) . The EK and SRK are open key cryptography key pairs. The TPM stores the private key of each of these key sets.

The endorsement key is the establishment of the root of trust for revealing the platform integrity. The endorsement key is created in the assembling procedure while manufacturing the TPM modules. An associated key particularly recognizes a stage, and in a perfect world, ought to stay unaltered for the duration of the life of the related TPM. Be that as it may, TPM sellers can uncover usefulness that permits an endorsement key to be changed (Grawrock, D., 2009). Taking responsibility or ownership privileges for TPM enables the stage proprietor to make a capacity root key match. In case of a change of access privileges of the ownership, the new TPM owner can create an alternate storage root key pair. The SRK is the base of the foundation of trust for storage.

The platform integrity can be violated if the endorsement key is using for the signing the target platform. The Attestation Identity Key (AIK) is generated by using the endorsement key, which verify the TPM without revealing the state of the communicating TPM. As per the suggestion from the trusted computing group the attestation identity keys should be stored in the persistent and non-volatile memory or storage.

Platform Configuration Register

To store the integrity of the target platform, the TPM provides finite set of registers called as *Platform Configuration Registers (PCRs)*. The PCR registers are volatile, which are used to store the secure hash code of the target platform until verify the integrity of the required resource in the given location of the system. In general, the platform configuration registers are sixteen, among 0-7 are reserved for TPM state usage and remaining register user specific by the operating system and/or application of the computer system. The platform configuration registers cannot be lost the information until the system lost the power supply as well as it is not possible to reset the registers. The operation on platform configuration register are read and write, the TCG provides special TPM commands to perform these operations while users needed on PCR (Trusted Computing Group, 2007b) & (Grawrock, D., 2009). Two types of data are stored in the platform configuration register such as measured and hash codes of the measured values or we can say that measured digests. The write operation is exclusively for the extending the present digest with update value and measured values of the system value or data can be extended. In the case of the hash code extending the hash codes are updated with present hash of the target platform.

Platform Configuration Registers extending operation takes the current PCR value, which is concatenate with the measured hash code of the platform. Finally, the hash code will be computed using the concatenation operation. Platform Configuration Registers extending operation can be presented in the below, here i represents the current platform configuration registers (Trusted Computing Group, 2007b) & (Grawrock, D., 2009) . The platform configuration registers are fixed length and optimizes the computation process by limiting the unbounded location of the storage portions. The advantages of the PCR are fixed storage and de-preservation for the hash code of the platform. This implies that fixed length PCR is used for unbounded number of extending operation on the target platform. This provides a flexible and optimal storage service form the platform configuration registers

Example for this attack is removing the measured entities from the platform configuration registers. Suppose entities A, B and C are involved in the computation of the measurement in root of trust integrity check. The following scenario will illustrate the attack, where B is executed after A and before C, wishes to delete the possible entries i.e., $x = H(A)||H(B)$ and $z = x||H(C)$. From the TCG, it impossible or infeasible to find the key pair. Therefore, it is highly impossible to remove the B i.e., $H(x)= H(y)$. Without influencing the result of $H(z)$. The platform configuration registers plays a vital role in remote attestation and secure virtual machine launch as well as it can protect the sensitive private data.

TPM Functionality

The properties and functionalities of Trusted Platform Module ensures the special and interesting security aspects such as sealed storage, transitive trust, and remote attestation. This subsection explains the set of functionalities in terms of the security aspects.

Transitive Trust

The main vision of the transitive trust is to provide a large set trustworthy possibility in the given cloud platform. The transitive trust can be mainly described with three steps: an initial process starts with root of trust that performs an integrity measurement of the cloud entities, that the cloud provider may wish to add to the trustworthy cloud environment. The transitive trust can be measured in terms of program code, which can be verified during the remote attestation process to address the trustworthiness of the cloud components (Trusted Computing Group, 2007b) & (Grawrock, D., 2009). After performing the integrity measurement, platform configuration registers are extended with root of trust concept with hashed values in platform configuration registers for the accountability and login details for the future references in cloud environment.

After extending the platform configuration registers, the root of trust can decide whether the target component is trustworthy or not, if the set of components or entities expands to include the functionality of the measured entity. This is iterative process, until the other entities are verified with the platform integrity of the cloud environment. The transitive trust provides a way to verify the application level platform verification as well as root of trust in cloud infrastructure.

Sealed Storage

Sealed storage is a process of securing the private or confidential information from illegal access. The sealed storage concept has two major operations: *sealing* and *unsealing*. The sealed storage concept merges the encryption scheme with integrity measurement to protect the target data and root of trust for storage(RTS) (Grawrock, D., 2009) . The sealing process takes two arguments as input such as sensitive data that we need to protect and respective platform configuration registers measurement digest. This process uses the storage key as encryption key, which would be taken from the storage root key tree. These steps are internal to the TPM, where storage root key is used to encrypt the respective platform configuration register measurement digest (Grawrock, D., 2009).

The sealing process encrypts platform configuration with the sealed data package that includes the both software and hardware components of the cloud platform. This means that the sealed facts can best be revealed while the platform is in the equal nation it was whilst the sealing operation occurred. This conduct is enforced via the inclusion of a nonce that only the TPM that executed the operation is aware of (Grawrock, D., 2009) & (Trusted Computing Group, 2011).

The unseal operation decrypts or recover the original information by using reverse operation of the seal operation. This unseal seal operation must be happen within the same TPM, where the seal operation performed. The unseal operation is successful if and if it must be decrypt with same TPM, same platform configuration register's measurement digest and data integrity should not be compromised.

The initial step is for the TPM to unseal the information within the sealed sensitive information bundle. This step includes all the operations such as decryption of sensitive information with correct storage key from the storage root key tree. Finally, this process reveals the measurement hash values in the respective platform configuration registers and nonce value.

The revealed measurement hash values and nonce are used to finish the operation. The nonce value will be matched with the internal TPM nonce value. If the TPM nonce is matched, then the TPM is responsible for creating the sealed data package. The success of theses operation results the protected data otherwise it sends fail signal (Grawrock, D., 2009) & (Trusted Computing Group, 2011).

Remote Attestation

Before launching the consumer virtual machine, cloud providers platform has to be verified using the remote attestation concept. If the platform is not trusty, consumer will not launch the virtual machine otherwise the consumer launches the virtual machine on top of the verified the platform. The remote attestation can be mainly divided into two major principle stages; those are used during the verification process.

One of these stages takes place on the platform under verification. This platform receives are quest for the execution of TPM's TPM_Quote command together with a set of platform configuration registers to quote, a once to prevent replay attacks, and the attestation identify key to use in the digital signature. Upon reception of this request the platform's TPM verifies the authorization to use the desired attestation identity key, creates a structure holding the measurement digests in the requested set of platform configuration registers, combines this information with the provided nonce, and produces a digital signature. The next stage takes place on the platform performing the verification. After requesting the quote operation, this platform receives a fresh digital signature of the desired platform configuration registers. The public key of the private-public attestation identity key pair is used to verify the signature, the AIK key itself is verified, and then the measurement digests are checked. This last step evaluates the trustworthiness of the remote platform, which can either be trustworthy or not (Grawrock, D., 2009) & (Trusted Computing Group, 2011).

RESEARCH DIRECTIONS

The above subsection explained about the insider attacks and external attacks in cloud computing environment. Many of the cloud service providers ignoring insider attacks because insiders are well sophisticated about the internal structure and they will have privileged access to perform their duties. The insiders take this scenario as an advantage to deploy their attacks on consumer resources in the cloud environment. The main motivation of this research is to prevent and detect the insider attacks in the cloud infrastructure using trusted cloud computing techniques. In this section, we will see about reasons to ignoring the problem

- Easy to implement
- High chance of success
- Ongoing solutions not accurate
- Less chance to detect and prevent

Easy to Implement

Insider attacks are easy to implement because insiders have sophisticated with internal structure of a cloud organization. Here, the chance of caught being very less when compared with the external attacks. The external attackers have no idea about internal structure of data systems of cloud organization and the chance of success is less than the internal attacks. Some insiders perform a straight forward attack due to their administrative legitimate access and well known structure about the cloud service provider data centers.

High Chance of Success

The insiders possibly have legitimate access and required permissions to login into the cloud service provider data centers. It is highly impossible to prevent them to access database while doing their duties and it is hard to detect these attacks. More case studies about insider threats tell us that insider threats are so easy to perform but external attacks make very difficult. The probability of insider attacks is very high because of its easiness to access the cloud resources. Even though, the cloud service provider maintaining proper access control and solid security policies, an insider attacks are easy to implement than external attacks.

Ongoing Solutions Not Accurate

Many of security devices are deployed to implement security policies and mechanisms to prevent the insider attacks and external attacks. The intrusion detection and prevention systems are deployed to detect and prevent such kind of behavior within the cloud. But, these algorithms and policies are working external attacks only; it doesn't pose any impact on insider threats. The firewalls are deployed to restrict the outside people to access the cloud resources but in case of insiders, firewalls cannot prevent them to access the insider to do attacks. Once an insider got access, they can disclose sensitive data to the intended people with available services e.g., through mail. These behaviors cannot be controlled by firewalls. Most of the intrusion detection and prevention systems are working on known signatures of attacks from the external sources only. It won't pose an impact on insider threats apart from this insider can compromise the firewalls. These security measures that are in place perimeter and do not scale to the insiders. The security and measures are hard to implement against the insiders in large cloud provider and scale is hard.

Less Chance to Detect and Prevent

In fact, the insider has legitimate access and sophisticated knowledge about company's data centers. The insider without bypassing the security policy; it is hard to detect and analysis and less chance to caught. If the insider has maliciously compromise the firewall and doing malicious things by bypassing the security policies, here the chance of caught is very high. The insider can perform attacks on what he has actual access rights. So, the chance of being caught is very hard and difficult.

Cloud provider can ensure data integrity and confidentiality by constantly storing cloud consumer data in encrypted format and the reverse operation i.e., decrypting the encrypted data within the same cloud platform. This work hypothesized that cloud service provider is malicious and cloud consumer is not having any security constraints to access their cloud assets. The model described in two locations in cloud infrastructure. This work hypothesized that legacy operating system with malicious insider at cloud platform. Such that, it clearly states that kernel and user mode is not modified apart from that an insider can compromise virtual machine's, those are running on controller of target cluster. For example, an insider can modify target virtual machines kernel and they can launch virtual machines with malicious intention without any permissions from consumer virtual machine. It leads to sensitive data breach of cloud storage of target virtual machines and neighbor virtual machine. With reference of this attack pattern, virtual machine's those are running on node controller are in great threat from insiders.

The cloud service provider contains ring 0 privileges to access any content of cloud consumers of physical resources hosted at cloud data center. To launch insider attack on resources, insider obtains a memory dump of target virtual machines. Initially malicious insider has no idea about credentials stored in dump of virtual machines kernel image. To obtain a password from memory snapshot, an attacker or insider simply devises a method on obtained dump of virtual machines. The memory dump filtered using strings command, it thoroughly checks dump and returns available strings with name of password. Once insider obtains credentials from kernel of virtual machines, the following are expected issues:

- A cloud service provider can access guest OS contents by using their privileges.

With effect of this cloud client might lose their data confidentiality and integrity. As said earlier, cloud service provider can save, restore, reboot, and shutdown any guest operating system.

- In (Rocha, F. and Correia, M., 2011) demonstrated various attack scenarios and those pose great threats in cloud computing virtual environment.

A malicious insider or malicious cloud service provider can alter or breach data upon agreed with competitors of the consumer company. Attackers with the cloud organization will have great vulnerabilities to sensitive information because they are sophisticated about internal structure. So, that cloud service providers have to ensure the data integrity and confidentiality of cloud consumer.

SUMMARY

This introduction provides definition of insider attacks in cloud computing with various basic security and design principles of virtualization. The trustworthy computing provides the basic information about how to provide the trust over the hosted resources in cloud ecosystem with TPM functionalities.

REFERENCES

Cappelli, D. M., Moore, A. P., & Trzeciak, R. F. (2012). *The CERT guide to insider threats: how to prevent, detect, and respond to information technology crimes (Theft, Sabotage, Fraud).* Addison-Wesley.

Darwish, M., Ouda, A., & Capretz, L. F. (2013, June). Cloud-based DDoS attacks and defenses. In *Information Society (i-Society), 2013 International Conference on* (pp. 67-71). IEEE.

Denning, P. J. (1971). Third generation computer systems. *ACM Computing Surveys*, *3*(4), 175–216. doi:10.1145/356593.356595

Goldberg, R. P. (1974). Survey of Virtual Machine Research. *IEEE Computer*, *7*(9), 34–45. doi:10.1109/MC.1974.6323581

Grawrock, D. (2009). *Dynamics of a Trusted Platform: A Building Block Approach.* Intel Press.

Greene, J. (2010). *Intel Trusted Execution Technology: Hardware-based Technology for Enhancing Server Platform Security. Technical report.* Intel.

Intel. (2014). *Hardware-Assisted Virtualization.* Author.

Kim, T., Peinado, M., & Mainar-Ruiz, G. (2012, August). STEALTHMEM: System-Level Protection Against Cache-Based Side Channel Attacks in the Cloud. In USENIX Security symposium (pp. 189-204). USENIX.

Mell, P., & Grance, T. (2011). *The NIST definition of cloud computing.* NIST.

Rocha, F., & Correia, M. (2011). *Lucy in the sky without diamonds: Stealing confidential data in the cloud. Proceedings of the 1*st *International Workshop on Dependability of Clouds, Data Centers and Virtual Computing Environments, DSNW '11.*

Romanosky, S., Telang, R., & Acquisti, A. (2011). Do data breach disclosure laws reduce identity theft? *Journal of Policy Analysis and Management*, *30*(2), 256–286. doi:10.1002/pam.20567

Scarfone, K. A., Souppaya, M. P., & Hoffman, P. (2011). *SP 800-125. Guide to Security for Full Virtualization Technologies. Technical report.* Gaithersburg, MD: National Institute of Standards and Technology.

Strongin, G. (2005). Trusted Computing Using AMD "Pacifica" and Presidio. Academic Press.

Trusted Computing Group. (2007b). *Trusted Computing Group–TCG Architecture Overview, Version 1.4*. Author.

Trusted Computing Group. (2011). *Trusted Computing Group - TPM Main Specification Level 2 Version 1.2, Revision 116: Part 3 -Commands*. Author.

Trusted Computing Group. (2014a). *Trusted Computing Group - AboutTCG*. Author.

Trusted Computing Group. (2014b). *Trusted Computing Group-Developers-FAQ*. Author.

VMWare. (2007). *Understanding Full Virtualization, Para virtualization, and Hardware Assist*. Retrieved from http://goo.gl/kfREyp

Whitaker, A., Shaw, M., & Gribble, S. (2002). Denali: Lightweight Virtual Machines for Distributed and Networked Applications. *Proceedings of the2002 USENIX Annual Technical Conference*.

Yan, Q., & Yu, F. R. (2015). Distributed denial of service attacks in software-defined networking with cloud computing. *IEEE Communications Magazine*, *53*(4), 52–59. doi:10.1109/MCOM.2015.7081075

Chapter 1
Security Architecture of Cloud Computing

ABSTRACT

Cloud computing is an innovation for dynamic resources to be used over the internet. Though cloud computing is cost effective and easy to use, security is often an area of concern. Sharing of sensitive information and running critical applications on public and/or shared cloud environments require high degree of security. Amount of data stored and processed is increasing enormously requiring cloud environments to resize to larger capacities. Cloud environments have both pros and cons concerning the security of data of the consumers using cloud services. This chapter discusses the main security issues faced by cloud computing environments. The main focus of this chapter is to describe the issues faced during building cross-domain collaborations over the internet and usage of cloud services and its security. This chapter also identifies the security at various levels of cloud computing and, based on cloud architecture, categorizes the security issues.

CLOUD COMPUTING SECURITY ARCHITECTURE

Cloud computing is service over the internet offering resources that can be dynamically scalable thus promising its adopters a lot of economic advantages. Cloud can be partitioned into different layers based on the type of resources provided. Bottom layer is Infrastructure-as-a-Service (IaaS) that provides the basic infrastructure components including Servers, CPUs, memory, and storage. Prominent examples of IaaS providers are Amazon Elastic Compute Cloud (EC2) and Amazon easy storage service (S3). The middle layer is Platform-as-a-service (PaaS) which deploys

DOI: 10.4018/978-1-5225-7924-3.ch001

applications of python, java, .net languages and also allows dynamic scaling of those applications. An example for PaaS is Google App Engine for net. Top most layer is allows cloud consumers to use the available applications and is referred to as Software-as-a-architecture (SaaS). SaaS has been globally accepted to access application functionality through a browser in a very trusted environment with no requirement to purchase or subscribe and install costly hardware or software. Two main technologies are currently used to access cloud services. Internet browsers are used for SaaS application access and .net technology services are for accessing IaaS services. Both the afore mentioned approaches can be found in PaaS environment. This chapter summarizes the security problems concerned with cloud computing.

Figure 1. Security architecture of cloud computing
(Mell, P., & Grance, T.,2011)

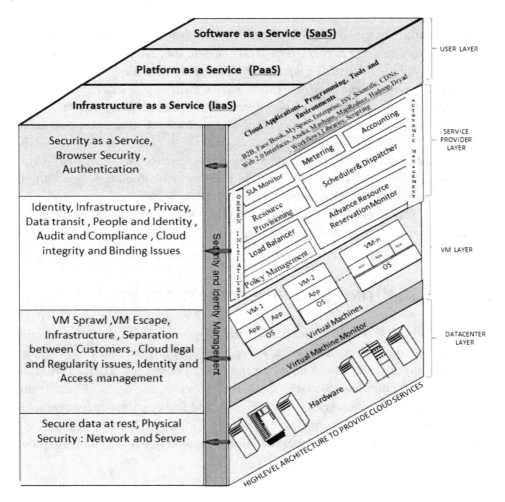

High-Level Overview of Cloud Architecture

This section gives the architectural view of security issues faced in cloud computing environment while providing security to consumers. Cloud computing services have been categorized into four layers depending on the three cloud computing resource categories viz. IaaS, SaaS and PaaS. We elaborate each of the four layers in this section and also map the various security issues in each layer as shown in Figure 1.

Important features of User layer are Cloud applications, environments, programming and tools. Few popular examples which come under this category are B2B, facebook, Myspace, Enterprise, ISV, scientific, CDNs, Web 2.0 interfaces, Aneka, Mashups, Map Reduce, Hadoop, Dyrad, Workflows, libraries, scripting. Security as a service, browser security and authentication are few of the security issues present in the user layer. They are discussed in detail in next section.

Few components of service provider layer are SLA monitoring, metering, accounting, resource provisioning, scheduler and dispatcher, load balancer, advance resource reservation monitor and policy management between costumers. Legal and regularity issues of cloud, access and identity management are components of Virtual machine (VM) layer. Important components of Data center (infrastructure) layer include servers, CPUs, memory, and storage. Main security issue of Data center layer is physical security: security of network and server.

Security of End User

End users should be informed about the access agreements including acceptable use or conflict of interest and should comply with them to access resources within the cloud. If a client organization finds vulnerable code or protocols at servers, firewalls, mobile devices or at other such entry points, they should have a mechanism to upload patches of such vulnerable code on native system as soon as they are found. And in turn cloud should secure its services from any user with malicious intent from gaining access to any information or services.

Security-as-a-Service

Cloud service providers (CSPs) provide security to cloud customers using cloud services. Security-as-a-Service is a cloud service to provide security and can be implemented in two ways; first method anybody can change the delivery methods including established information security vendors; in the second method, cloud service providers themselves provide security as part of cloud service (Varadharajan, V., & Tupakula, U., 2014).

Browser Security

Remote servers perform computations in a cloud environment. Authorizing and authenticating information to cloud and performing input/output operations are the tasks carried out at the client side. World throughout, client software used by all customers is a platform independent standard web browser. This software can be of various types; Software-as-a-Service (SaaS), Web applications, or web 2.0. Data encryption and host authentication is performed using Transport layer security (TLS). TLS is used to protect data during transport as well as for authentication of server's domain name.

The Legacy Same Origin Policy is used to add scripting languages to web pages. The policy allows read or write operations on content to request from same origin and disallow access on content from any other different origin.

Browser based cloud authentication is a security concern as the browser based protocols are weak because they are not capable of generating cryptographically valid XML tokens. Hence the task is assigned to a trusted third party. User login is not verified at server as browser has very few credentials and so HTTP forwards the user id and password to the passport login server. The credentials then is converted to Kerberos token which is redirected to the requesting server. At this point any potential attacker can access these tokens which can lead to the attacker getting access to all of the services of the victim. Browser based authentication can be improved by combining TLS and SOP. Also the browser security API can be enhanced by adding XML encryption and XML signature by loading appropriate java scripts into the library at runtime(Ramgovind, S., et. al.,, 2010).

Authentication

Due to advent of internet and cloud computing, today all data over the cloud is accessible anywhere anytime for anybody making access control more important than ever before. User authentication is the primary basis for access control in cloud environments. Trusted Platform Module (TPM) is available widely with its authentication capability stronger than usernames and passwords. IF-MAP (Interface for Metadata Access Points) is an open specification developed by Trusted Computing Group (TCG) used to perform real time communication between cloud provider and customer on information regarding authorized users and other security issues. For example, in a scenario when a user is reassigned or fired, the cloud provider can be informed in real-time by the customer uniqueness management system so that the particular user's access can be modified or revoked immediately. In such a case if the fired user tries to access the cloud, permission would be denied.

SERVICE PROVIDER SECURITY ISSUES

Cloud supplier should make sure that a cloud computing resolution satisfies organizational security and privacy protocols while offering public cloud computing environment. Additionally cloud supplier must provide proof of effectiveness of the security controls necessary while migrating organizational information and functions into the cloud (Zissis, D., & Lekkas, D.,2012).

Identity and Access Management

Authorization, Authentication and Auditing (AAA) of users accessing cloud services are the features of Identity and access management (IAM). Usually organizations have a mostly static "trust boundary" which is monitored and controlled for applications deployed within the perimeter of the organization. Whereas in a private data center, trust boundary encompasses the networks, systems and applications. Such centers are secured via network security controls which include prevention systems(IPSs), intrusion detection systems (IDSs), virtual private numbers (VPNs) and multifactor authentication. (Ferris, J. M. 2011). In cloud computing environment, organization's trust boundary becomes dynamic and the applications, system, and network boundary of an organization

Privacy

Privacy is one of the most important issue in security of cloud computing. Regulations regarding personal information storage and the number of restrictions placed by various countries varies across the world. In any jurisdiction, a single level of service is acceptable for a cloud service provider. It is difficult to authenticate the data if it is stored based on contractual commitments for privacy regulations in few countries. As the quantity of private and confidential data is increasing in huge quantity, an effective assessment strategy is required which should cover data protection, privacy, compliance, identity management, secure operations, and other related legal security issues.

SECURING DATA IN TRANSMISSION

Data transmission uses encryption techniques to protect data integrity and make sure data is delivered to the customer and is not modified in transmission. These techniques use SSL/TLS protocols. In any application, data to be processed should be in decrypted format. Man in middle attack is a type of cryptographic attack which happens when an attacker places himself in the path of data transmission. Thus to maintain confidentiality and integrity of data-in-transmission to and from cloud provider advanced cryptographic encryption schemes must be used which allow data to be processed without being decrypted.

User Identity

In an organizational setup, users who are authorized can access the organizational enterprise, data and tools whenever required and those not authorized will not get permission for access. Cloud setup is similar with the difference that a cloud environment supports a large enterprise and various communities of users making cloud controls all the more critical. Administrators are a level of privileged users working for the cloud provider. The task of administrators is user monitoring including logging activities. Background checking and physical monitoring are part of user monitoring. Enterprise backend or third party systems are used for coordinating authentication and authorization by having rapid on boarding capabilities. Single sign on capabilities provide users easy and quick leverage to cloud services by simplifying user logons on both internally hosted applications and the cloud.

Audit and Compliance

Audit and compliance to internal and external processes must be carried out by an organization which should stand with the requirements of customer contracts, laws and regulations, internal corporate policies which are driven by business objectives and monitor them without fail. In traditional outsourcing, relationships play a very important role for audit and compliance. Under the dynamic nature of cloud, PaaS, SaaS, IaaS environment functions increase in importance.

In cloud, audit and compliance is performed with coordination of external auditing, regulatory compliance and internal policy compliance.

CLOUD INTEGRITY AND BINDING ISSUES

Cloud malware injection attack is a type of attack in cloud system for injecting a malicious service program or virtual machine. It results in data modifications to full functionality changes or blockings. Major task of cloud computing systems is to coordinate and maintain instances of virtual machines (IaaS) or explicit service execution modules (PaaS).

Flooding Attacks

Cloud system provider maintains all basic operational tasks in Cloud Computing. In this tasks server hardware maintenance is the most important instead of operating as own hardware. So, Cloud Computing enables companies (clients) to *rent* server hardware on demand (IaaS). It gives more economic benefits when it comes to dynamics in server load. Same servers can operate in different time zones with different data traffic. In Cloud Computing environment provides a dynamic adaptation of hardware requirements to the actual workload occurring without buying sufficient server hardware for the high workload times. Practically, it can be achieved by using virtual machines. If a company's demand on computational power rises, it simply is provided with more instances of virtual machines for its services.

Direct Denial of Service is a service attack involves saturating the objective with bogus requests to prevent it from responding to reasonable requests in a timely manner. An attacker to launch physical attack typically uses multiple computers or a botnet. It can capture large number of resources to protect against and cause charges to rise. The cloud dynamic provisioning in some ways minimizes the task of an attacker to cause harm. At the same time, the resources of a cloud are significant with enough attacking computers they can become saturated. *Indirect Denial of Service* is manage the computational power of the attacker, in cloud service the direct flooding attack gives some side effect and the same hardware provides some other services may suffer the workload caused by the flooding (Osanaiye, O., et al., 2016).

The service instance may on flooded service instance, the same server with another. By using the flooding attack requests the server's hardware resources are completely exhausted, then the same hardware machine are unable to perform the other service instances intended tasks. So, the Denial of Service is targeted other services with target service instances on the same server hardware. In Cloud computing environment, denial of service can cause and notice the lack of availability and switch to other service instances to other servers. It is extra burden to all other servers and it spreads all the servers in the complete computing Cloud.

ACCOUNTING AND ACCOUNTABILITY

Accounting and Accountability is a main cost-effective driver behind operation a Cloud Computing service is charging the customers according to their actual usage and another flooding attack on a Cloud service is drastically increasing the bills for Cloud usage. For computational power usage there is no "upper limits" then the client running the flooded service most likely has to foot the bill for the workload caused by the attacker

Security Issues in Virtualization

Generally the software implementation of a machine that executes programs like a physical machine is a Virtual Machine(VM). The lowest common denominator to impact the safety of all is extending virtual machines to public clouds which causes the enterprise network perimeter to evaporate (Popović, K., & Hocenski, Ž. 2010, May).

VM Escape

If VM is improperly configured this could allow functionality to fully avoid the virtual environment, as a result it leads to full system failure in the security mechanisms and is known as VM Escape. Hypervisor the part of VM that enables VM/host isolation and resource sharing are some more risks in VM. Necessary separation during planned attack which greatly determines how the VM can continue to exist risk is provided. Rogue Hypervisors is the guest OS which is booted inside a virtual environment like a traditional OS. Managing network traffic. Not only in the VM but also on the host machine the hypervisor has a full control over the system. The treat of denial-of-service(DoS) attacks against a virtualized system is as common as is against no virtualized systems. As the VM share host's resources, a denial of service attacks against another VM, the host, or an external service is actually greatly increased.

VM Security Recommendations Best Practice Security Techniques

Vulnerabilities are moved to the virtual machine OS from the OS of the host computer and is known as Hardening. To avoid intruders from attacking the hardware we can limit the physical access to the host, which in turn protect the hardware of VM. Cryptography techniques like Transport Layer Security(TLS), encrypted Virtual Private Network(VPN),Secure Shell(SSH)etc.. can be used for encrypted communication between client domain and host domain. Low priority processes can be scheduled to run after important hours by disabling background tasks. The disturbance into the system can be checked by implementing file integrity checks. Strong authentication practice should be employed and use encrypted communications only such as a SSH or VPNs and MAC address or IP address filtering.

Separation Between Users

Separation between cloud provider's users is one of the most important cloud concern in order to avoid intentional or inadvertent access to sensitive information. VM and hypervisor are used separate cloud customers in a cloud environment. TPM provides VM integrity and hardware based verification and TNC architecture provides strong network separation and security.

Cloud Legal Issues

Regulatory and legal issues are addressed by practices and policies by a cloud provider, to ensure the adequacy each customer must have its legal and regulatory experts. The issues to be considered include auditing, data security and export. TPM and trusted storage techniques can play a key role in limiting data access.

Infrastructure Security Issues

Security related services are provided to a good vary of client types by cloud suppliers, the security is created on the market to those with the smallest amount stringent necessities. For effectiveness the infrastructure security solutions should be a part of an entire and secure design (Hashizume, K., et.al., 2013).

Securing Data Storage

Environment data protection which concerns with the way which data is accessed, stored, audit requirements, compliance, notification requirements, issues involving the cost of data breaches, and damage to brand value is the most important security issue in Cloud Computing. Regulated and sensitive data needs to be properly segregated in the service provider's datacenter in the cloud storage infrastructure. By using encryption and managing encryption keys of data in transfer to the cloud we can protect data privacy and manage compliance which are very critical. Cloud service provider and Consumer share a secure encryption key, Encryption of mobile media which is very important is often overlooked.

PaaS, Data at rest applications are economics of cloud computing and a multitenancy architecture used in SaaS. Data is commingled with other user's data when stored by a cloud based application, or processed by a cloud-based application. Data co-location has some significant restrictions in Cloud Computing. The cloud wide data classification will govern how that data is encrypted, who has access and archived, and how technologies are used to prevent loss in public and financial services areas involving users and data with different risks. Cryptographic encryption is the

9

best practice for securing data at rest at the cloud provider, Hard drive manufacturers use shipping self-encryption. Automated encryption with minimal cost impact is provided by Self-encryption compared to Software encryption which is less secure and slower as the encryption key can be copied off the machine with detection.

Network and Server

Server-side Protection: Unlike non-virtual counterparts, Virtual servers and applications have to be compelled to be secured in IaaS clouds. Teams of virtual machines are isolated from hosted teams by virtual firewalls, liked production systems from development systems or development systems from different cloud resident systems. To avoid accidental deploying of pictures underneath development or containing vulnerabilities, rigorous managing of virtual machine pictures is vital. In hybrid cloud which is a sort of composite cloud with similar protection problems, the infrastructure consists of private cloud composed with either public cloud or another organization's private cloud. The clouds staying as distinctive entities permits unified service delivery, however it additionally creates interdependency. Example, identification and authentication performed through an organization's personal cloud infrastructure, as a method for its users to achieve access to services provisional in a very public cloud. The major concern with hybrid clouds is preventing holes or leaks between the composed infrastructures, as a result this will increase in complexity and diffusion of responsibilities. The availability suffers proportionately with the availability % drops. A purchaser wish the talent to configure policy-based security zone or virtual domain. As data moves beyond client's management, they expect capabilities like intrusion detection and prevention. Intrusions into a client's trusted virtual domain is not a sole priority, but the potential for data leakages. For extrusions-the misuse of a client's domain to mount attacks on third parties. Moving data raises additional problems regarding internal and Internet based denial of service(DoS) or distributed denial of service(DDoS) attacks. All parties should agree on their responsibilities to review data in a shared environment. The organization to take lead in terms of contract management for any risk assessments and does not execute directly. Cloud provider provides image catalogs, purchasers want this to be secured and protected against corruption and abuse. To take care of software security, most of the enterprises with data security programs institute security program. The existing application security programs need to reevaluate current practices and standards for designing and implementing applications targeted for deployment on a cloud.

REFERENCES

Ferris, J. M. (2011). *U.S. Patent No. 7,886,038*. Washington, DC: U.S. Patent and Trademark Office.

Hashizume, K., Rosado, D. G., Fernández-Medina, E., & Fernandez, E. B. (2013). An analysis of security issues for cloud computing. *Journal of Internet Services and Applications*, 4(1), 5. doi:10.1186/1869-0238-4-5

Osanaiye, O., Choo, K. K. R., & Dlodlo, M. (2016). Distributed denial of service (DDoS) resilience in cloud: Review and conceptual cloud DDoS mitigation framework. *Journal of Network and Computer Applications*, 67, 147–165. doi:10.1016/j.jnca.2016.01.001

Popović, K., & Hocenski, Ž. (2010, May). Cloud computing security issues and challenges. In *MIPRO, 2010 proceedings of the 33rd international convention* (pp. 344-349). IEEE.

Ramgovind, S., Eloff, M. M., & Smith, E. (2010, August). The management of security in cloud computing. In Information Security for South Africa (ISSA), 2010 (pp. 1-7). IEEE. doi:10.1109/ISSA.2010.5588290

Varadharajan, V., & Tupakula, U. (2014). Security as a service model for cloud environment. *IEEE eTransactions on Network and Service Management*, 11(1), 60–75. doi:10.1109/TNSM.2014.041614.120394

Zissis, D., & Lekkas, D. (2012). Addressing cloud computing security issues. *Future Generation Computer Systems*, 28(3), 583–592. doi:10.1016/j.future.2010.12.006

Chapter 2
Trusted Cloud Computing

ABSTRACT

This chapter introduces various ideas to deal with insider attacks using the research directions, which are discussed in earlier chapters such as remote attestation, sealed storage, and integrity measurement. Trusted computing dependent on hardware root of trust has been produced by industry to secure computing frameworks and billions of end points. Remote attestation provides a facility to attestation the required platforms using platform configuration registers (PCR), and sealed storage is used to encrypt the consumer sensitive data using cryptographic operations. Integrity measurements are used to measure the given computing components in respective register. Here, the authors concentrated on a trusted computing paradigm to enable cloud service providers to solve the potential insider attacks at cloud premises.

TRADITIONAL COMPUTING

As computing develops, the lines isolating a significant number of the traditional computing environments are obscuring. Consider the "ordinary office environment". Just a couple of years prior, this condition comprised of PCs associated with a network, with servers giving files and printing services. Remote access was clumsy, and versatility was accomplished by utilization of laptops and smart phones. Terminals appended to centralized computers (main frames) were predominant at numerous organizations too, with even less remote access and portability alternatives. The current pattern is toward giving more approaches to access these computing environments. Web technologies and others like it are extending the limits of traditional computing. Organizations build up portals, which give web openness to their inside servers.

DOI: 10.4018/978-1-5225-7924-3.ch002

Network computers are basically terminals that comprehend web-based computing. Hand held PCs can synchronize with other PCs to permit extremely versatile utilization of organization data. Hand held PDAs can connect with remote systems to utilize the organization's web-based interface and other web resources. At home, most clients had a solitary PC with a slower modem association with the workplace, the Internet, or both. Today, network speeds once accessible at an extraordinary expense are generally modest, giving home clients access to more information. These quick network and data connections are enabling home PCs to present pages and to run networks that incorporate printers, customer PCs, and servers. A few homes even have firewalls to shield their systems from security breaks. Those firewalls cost a huge number of dollars a couple of years prior and did not even exist 10 years back. In the last half of the earlier century, computing assets were rare.

For a certain time, frameworks were either batch or interactive. Batch frameworks processed jobs in bulk, with foreordained inputs (from records or different wellsprings of information). Intelligent or interactive frameworks sat tight for inputs from clients. To streamline the utilization of the computers, various clients shared time on these frameworks. Time-sharing frameworks utilized timers and scheduling algorithms to quickly cycle processes through the CPU, giving every client a share of the assets. Today, conventional time-sharing frameworks are uncommon. A similar booking procedure is still being used on workstations and servers, however as often as possible the processes are altogether belonging to the same client (or a solitary client and the working framework). Client processes, and framework processes that provide services to the client, are overseen with the goal that each often gets a cut of computer time. Consider the windows made while a client is working on a PC, for instance, and the fact that they might perform distinctive tasks in the same time.

Organizations with this IT model must buy extra equipment and upgrades with the end goal to scale up their data storage and services to help more clients. Software upgrades are a must and are additionally required with traditional IT framework to guarantee fail safe systems are set up on the off chance that an equipment failure happens. For some organizations with IT data centers, an in-house IT department is expected to install and keep up (maintain) the equipment.

Then again, conventional IT frameworks are viewed as a standout amongst the most secure data facilitating solutions and enables you to keep up full control of your organization's applications and data on the local server. They are a customized, devoted system perfect for organizations that need to run various sorts of applications.

DRAWBACKS IN TRADITIONAL COMPUTING

Even though the traditional computing served up as the kick starter the IT age or computer revolution and replaced the conventional paper file systems it has its own drawbacks. Some of the drawbacks are explained below.

Deployment of Traditional IT Services

When you deploy a new service, traditional IT necessitates that you buy another program for that service. Your organization pays a forthright expense, and afterward you possess this program. Enlisted IT personnel at that point load the program onto the computers in the framework, which can take some time contingent upon the idea of the service to be deployed and in addition the size and schedule of your IT group.

Upgrades in Traditional IT Service

Traditional IT requires your IT group to invest a lot of time and energy administrating an upgrade, upgrading methods that take significantly less time are needed.

Scalability of Traditional IT Services

When you buy a traditional IT service, you buy what you require at the same time. This includes some estimation and anticipating on your part. Imagine a scenario where your necessities change over time? Technology with great scalability and flexibility is required for the organizations that may experience changes and need more, less, or distinctive services later.

The Cost of Traditional IT Services

At the point when business choices are made, cost is dependably a contributing element. With traditional IT your organization buys what you require forthright and depending upon what you are buying this can be a sizable measure of cash. Sometime later you buy upgrades for your technology services to make it faster and better, until the point that it can never again be overhauled. At the point when your buy winds up inoperable or terminated, then you must make another expensive buy.

Data Storage in Traditional IT Services

The requirement for storage has grown exponentially through the years. Traditionally, an organization would need to suit for these developing data storage needs in-house.

If your organization has long haul associations with customers that include record keeping, for example, a doctor-patient relationship or a relationship that includes monetary record keeping over time, at that point space for putting information for a long period of time turns into a critical issue. With traditional data storage techniques, space is constrained. A technology that alleviates this problem is very much required.

Backups in Traditional IT Services

Everyone's worry with technology is how to shield their vital data safe from being lost or decimated in a catastrophic event, otherwise natural disasters. With traditional IT, would you be able to make sure that your organization's sensitive and The rapid advancement of science and technology in other areas demanded engineers to come up with new ideas that alleviate the drawbacks of traditional computing. And from these new ideas came a new form of computing that would go on to become the backbone of AI Revolution and it is called Cloud Computing.

CLOUD IN THE ASCENDENCY

Cloud computing is the popular expression now in the field of information technology. It is the idea of where an association has its information and applications facilitated on a third- party infrastructure. Occasionally the applications are structured and created by the service providers and the organization utilizing it utilizes that application against its own information. There are a few elements for rule for it and in addition a few factors that bring up solid issues for its acknowledgment. It is completely founded on the need of the association, regardless of whether it use cloud computing or not. Cloud is an innovation with stupendous social, scientific, and business benefits. Early stage cloud computing was a lot of technical than it's currently-something that IT departments at the time were well used to. Anyone who has a good knowledge on virtual engines were able to set up cloud environment. At first, cloud started off by offering basic services like storage, compute and network. Over the last ten years, we've got seen the amount of information hold on within the cloud grow exponentially with businesses often handling petabytes of information, compared to the gigabytes of time.

As data volumes grew and users grew, cloud suppliers began to supply a lot of cloud- based added services. Cloud usage has been increased these days in such a way that the purchasing of cloud is no longer confined to IT. In real sense, the cloud is regarding democratization and equality, giving individuals a voice, and additionally the ability to urge things done. The Figure 1 shows the cloud computing execution scenario in an abstract way.

Figure 1. Cloud computing scenario

The cloud is already impacting our lives in several ways and fascinating trends that are taking form across wide areas of society. You may have heard of the One laptop per child (OLPC) initiative, geared toward planning a pc low-cost enough to be available of kids from the world's poor countries. It was a noble plan, however unable to measure up to expectations. It had been a hardware-focused read of the globe, engineered with non-standard technology that was unfamiliar to individuals outside the science laboratory wherever it had been designed. A significant substance was the restricted choice of software package obtainable, additionally to distribute it, a way to install it, a way to maintain it, and what licensing was needed. New communications models like blogs and Facebook have toppled governments, launched and unsuccessful merchandise, engineered and ruined reputations and given everyone a voice. currently everybody has their own machine, their own electro-acoustic transducer, their own station to unfold their message to the globe.

The cloud has upended traditional communication models, and the world is ever- changing as a result. In the past, communications were one-to-many, whether for newspapers, radio, TV. It absolutely was the method firms offer data concerning their product and governments communicated with the public. Today the model has been inverted: currently we've got many-to-one communication (think Twitter and Facebook), wherever the page owner will issue a message, and a whole bunch, thousands or variant folks will respond. The result's a brand-new transparency as folks communicate with politicians, pop stars and anyone on the public stage during a very open way.

Another area where the cloud is creating a sway is education, where innovative teaching tools and reference materials enable educators to stretch their precious budgets. For instance, think about a tool like Google Earth – it's not simply a geographic resource; students and academics will augment it with photos and links from their community. It's possible for anyone with an online association to urge high-quality instruction at any level. One nice example is that the Khan Academy (www.khanacademy.org), dedicated to providing "a free foremost education to anyone anyplace." With thousands of instructional videos, beside tests and teaching aids, it's the biggest assortment of instruction on the net. Content is delivered in a very informal vogue in 10-20-minute chunks designed for the net that are far more participating than a typical video of a physical lecture. Years ago, if you walked into an applied science laboratory, you'd see strain gages, gears, motors, and so on. In a technology science lab, you'd see board circuits and oscilloscopes. In an exceedingly chemical engineering science lab, you'd notice beakers and Bunsen burners. Today, in any engineering science lab despite specialty, you'll doubtlessly visualize racks of computers since the complexness of today's scientific and engineering issues is much on the far side the capabilities of ancient tools. Breakthroughs area unit supported modeling and simulation that need huge amounts of computing power. The cloud provides prepared access to it power, on an extremely economical pay-as-you-go basis.

Some of us can remember the first days of computing, where everybody had a 'dumb terminal' that was connected to a mainframe for process and storage. Then within the eighties, the laptop brought processors and storage to our fingertips, providing the focus of innovation that lasted decades. currently the apparatus has shifted once more, with data, applications, and computing power re-centralized to create those resources accessible to everybody. However, in contrast to within the past, the cloud permits users – individual, companies, and international communities – nearly unlimited ability in how they how benefit of it.

The result is an explosion of innovation with tremendous social, scientific, and business edges. The foremost exciting factor is that the developments represented here area unit simply the start.

HOW CAN THE CLOUD TRANSFORM YOUR ORGANIZATION?

Flexibility

Scale up and right down to meet your organization's necessities. In today's economy, this flexibility is vital. you'll regulate your IT expenditures to fulfill your organization's immediate desires. You now not ought to build for the longer term or be affected by selections created or contracts signed within the past.

Security

Rest assured that your information within the cloud is far safer than what lives on a tower underneath your table or in your little unsecured server space.

Capacity

In the past, you had to pay tons of your IT budget on human resources to manage your software system. With cloud computing, that's not a problem. Now, you'll be able to concentrate on however the answer can assist you any your mission. The IT piece belongs to someone else.

Cost

Using cloud technology reduces your maintenance fees. No more servers, software, and update fees. many of the hidden prices generally related to code implementation, customization, hardware, maintenance, and coaching area unit rolled into a clear subscription fee.

It's Open

Internet standards and internet services enable you to attach services to every alternative. This implies that you just will alter your data and access it from anyplace within the world, on any laptop or mobile device, at any time. Even though hardware is consistently obtaining smaller, quicker and more powerful, and the demand for process power, storage space and data normally is growing and perpetually threatening to outstrip companies' skills to deliver.

With information being created in colossal sum through particular sources, the greatest change before the association today is to oversee them. In any case, computing gadgets, storing gadgets and other equipment are getting littler, incredible and quicker, the consistently developing measure of data has expanded the interest of processing power and storage limit and so on.

Significance of data center comes in the viewpoint of overseeing data created by associations, be it media transmission, educational institutions, money related establishments, web-based advertising or web based life Websites. According to an investigation, about 1.8 trillion GB of data was created in year 2011 alone and is relied upon to contact 40 ZB stamp continuously 2020.

In this way, associations require data centers to accumulate data on servers with the goal that it very well may be gotten to by any client sitting in any side of the globe by means of Internet empowered gadgets.

TRUSTED COMPUTING IN CLOUD

Trusted Computing Group

The Trusted Computing Group is a group collectively formed by AMD, Hewlett-Packard, IBM, Intel and Microsoft to execute Trusted Computing ideas across PCs. The Trusted Computing Group was declared in 2003 as the successor to the Trusted Computing Platform Alliance which was previously framed in 1999. Trusted Computing dependent on hardware root of trust has been produced by industry to secure computing frameworks and billions of end points.

TCG made the Trusted Platform Module cryptographic ability, which enforces particular practices and ensures that the system is protected from unapproved changes and attacks, for example, malware and root kits. As computing has extended to various gadgets and framework has advanced, so too has TCG expanded the idea of trusted frameworks well past the computer-with-a-TPM to different gadgets, from HDDs and cell phones.

Standards-based Trusted Computing advances created by TCG individuals presently are used in big business frameworks, enterprise systems, storage systems, networks, embedded systems, and mobile devices and can secure cloud computing and virtualized frameworks. A great many sellers offer an assortment of Trusted Computing-based products, including equipment, applications, and services.

The outcome is that frameworks, networks, and applications are more secure, less inclined to infections and malware and in this way more solid as well as more straightforward to deploy and less demanding to oversee.

Through open norms and specifications, Trusted Computing Group (TCG) empowers secure computing. Advantages of TCG technologies incorporate insurance of business-critical information and frameworks, secure validation and solid assurance of client personalities, and the foundation of solid machine identity and network integrity. Trusted equipment and applications decrease undertaking absolute expense of ownership and bolster administrative consistence.

Through its member-driven work groups, TCG empowers the advantages of trust in computing gadgets from portable to embedded systems, and in networks, storage, infrastructure, and cloud security. In excess of a billion gadgets incorporate TCG technologies. Essentially all enterprise PCs, numerous servers and and embedded systems incorporate the TPM; while networking hardware, drives and different gadgets a nd frameworks follow other TCG particulars, including self-encrypting drives and network security specifications.

Trusted Platform Module

A Trusted Platform Module (TPM) is a specialized chip on a computing device that stores RSA encryption keys particular to the host framework for authentication of hardware. TPM is a trusted hardware used for remote attestation to provide the integrity of a system and guarantee the trustworthiness of remote parties. It is tamper resistant security co-processor. Examples include Microsoft's BitLocker and HP's HP ProtectTools. The TPM has the following capabilities:

- Performing public key cryptographic operations and computing hash functions
- Key management and generation
- Secure storage of keys and other secret data
- Random number generation
- Integrity measurement
- Attestation

Each TPM chip has an Endorsement Key (EK) which is an RSA key pair. This pair is kept up inside the chip and cannot be tampered or accessed by code. The EK is unique to a TPM and is signed by a trusted Certification Authority (CA). The Storage Root Key (SRK) is made when a client or manager takes framework ownership. This key pair is produced by the TPM, dependent on the Endorsement Key and the password kept by the owner.

A second key, called an Attestation Identity Key (AIK) ensures the gadget against unapproved firmware and software modification by hashing sensitive segments of firmware and software before they are executed. At the point when the framework endeavors to connect with the network, the hashes are sent to a server that confirms that they equal expected values. On the off chance that any of the hashed segments has been altered since last boot, the match will fall flat, and the framework cannot enter the network.

TPM chips can be utilized with any major OS and work best when assisted by other security methods, for example, firewalls, antivirus and biometric check. In this way TPM ensures protection to the host system from a variety of attacks using *Trusted Computing*.

Figure 2. TPM root of trust

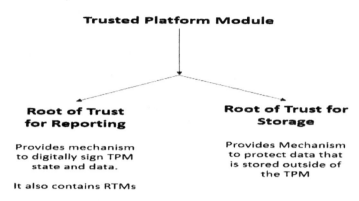

Trusted Platform Module

**Root of Trust
for Reporting**

Provides mechanism
to digitally sign TPM
state and data.

It also contains RTMs

**Root of Trust for
Storage**

Provides Mechanism
to protect data that
is stored outside of
the TPM

Root of Trust for Measurements

All root of trust measurements is not created equal. Root of Trust for Measurement (RTM) and Core RTM (CRTM) inside this detail allude to those elements that are related with the Host Platform. The RTM is certainly trusted. Trust in this part might be communicated through the Host Platform Certificate. The RTM is the point from which all trust in the measurement procedure is predicated. The RTM incorporates a center part called core component (the CRTM), the computing engine to run the core component, and the physical associations of the 45 cores and the computing engine.

Each component is measured before the control is passed to that component. It is called "Chain of Trust". The component of the RTM from which the begins the execution of the trusted states is called Core Root of Trust for Measurement. This measures the BIOS and itself and it is often termed as 'anchor' of the chain of trust. This detects things that change any of these critical boot time components like, MBR based root-kits or even BIOS attackers.

There are two types of root of trust measurements. Static Root of Trust for Measurement and Dynamic Root of Trust for Measurement. SRTM measures the same component every time at the boot time. DRTM measures different things every boot time. Virtualization is the backbone of cloud computing. It enables us to run different machines on a single machine and enables remote attestation. Over the past few years, the use of this technology grew exponentially with the growth of cloud computing. Because of its widespread adoption, it became a victim of several insider and outsider attacks. Outsider attacks are launched by external entities by exploiting the weaknesses in infrastructures and the insider attacks are the result of either intentional or unintentional mistakes by cloud administrators. A recent example of an outsider attack is a bad USB attack. The clients need to completely trust the

CSP to provide confidentiality and integrity to their private and very sensitive data. But recent developments in the attacks on cloud suggest otherwise.

Trusted Computing Group stepped forward and established certain measures to be followed and the algorithms to be applied but, these are not suited for the cloud environment. These algorithms are the same for all the different levels of protection, i.e., there are no different levels of protection. The second issue is, they are computationally infeasible for both the cloud and the clients (mostly thin clients). It is necessary to improve the security features of the cloud that would help in its growth and widespread adoption.

In this chapter, we discussed a thin client friendly framework that ranks the cloud providers based on their trust level and establishes trust between clients and CSPs and we check whether it is computationally feasible or not. In the first step, this framework attests, ranks, and then registers the cloud platform with the TP using the TPM (Trusted Platform Module) based attestation. In the second step, the client then selects the cloud platform according to its security needs and verifies through the TP the security guarantees of the platform.

APPROACH BASED ON RANKING

There are two main components in this framework, Node Controller (NC) and Cloud Controller (CC) and the two main entities are clients and the cloud providers and additionally, we have a Trusted Third Party that builds trust between the client and the CSP.

All the cloud service providers first need to attest their cloud with the trusted third party (TP). Once they are registered, they will be given a ranking and are allocated to a certain type of clouds that are differentiated based on the level of protection and security they are offering for the client's data. The table that is used by the third party to differentiate the clouds is shown in Figure 3.

Security is an important part of computing, especially if it is cloud computing. All the clients don't trust the cloud service provider the same way. And all the clients won't have the same level of data sensitivity. So, differentiating the cloud service providers based on the level of protection provided and type of clients that may want choose those services will be a good way for the client to choose a service provider based on his requirements which can also be cost effective.

In the Table 1, the organizations that have very sensitive data and that organizations that do not trust the Cloud Service Provider like Health care, military and government organizations can opt for "*Type A*" cloud that provides trusted execution from BIOS up to the application level. It continually monitors everything so that sensitive information won't be leaked. And the level of protection offered will decrease

Figure 3. TPM based execution environment
(Khan, I et.al., 2018)

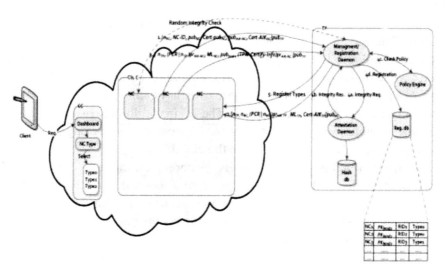

Table 1. Types of node controllers

NC Rank	NC's Attestation and Verification of Modules	Level of Protection Provided	Clients That Can Use This Service
Type A	BIOS, Bootloader, Virtual Machine Monitor, dom0 kernel and DRTM support from the inside of the VM	Trusted platform from BIOS up to application level. Thwarts rootkits and malware.	Client organizations that have very sensitive data and that have no trust in the CSP.
Type B	Attestation of SMM module and support for DRTM support from the inside of the VM.	No information about VMM, dom0 kernel. Security inside VM can be achieved through DRTM based isolated execution environment.	Client organizations that have very sensitive data and that have no trust in the CSP.
Type C	Attestation of BIOS, boot-loader, Virtual Machine Monitor and dom0 kernel	Trusted platform from BIOS to dom0 kernel.	Client organization that have little trust in the CSP
Type D	Attestation of dom-0 kernel and Virtual Machine Monitor.	Attestation of only virtualization layer above BIOS.	Client organization that have medium trust in the CSP.
Type E	No verification, platform is assumed to be trusted.	The software stack provided by the provider is trusted without any verification.	Client organization that completely trusts the CSP or that doesn't have any sensitive data.

(Khan, I et.al., 2018)

gradually as we progress further down the table with *"Type E"* providing the least security which is used by individuals mostly Node Controller Ranking.

Trust is the cornerstone for any distributed computing model especially cloud computing. The trust level a client shows varies on the type of data that he/she is uploading to the cloud. The client with data that is not so sensitive might completely trust the CSP with the security, but, government organizations like health, finance, military, NASA etc. have data that is so sensitive they cannot afford even a slightest of possibility that an attack can happen. These clients do not trust the CSP with their security features and check whether the CSP can provide strong isolation and transparency before moving their data to the cloud.

This framework defines five NC levels depending on the level of security that they will be providing. The NC levels go from Type-A through to Type-E with Type-A being most secure. Type-A platform calculates the static root of trust for measurement (SRTM) and the dynamic root of trust for measurement (DRTM), to provide dynamic runtime protection for client data and computation even from the cloud administrator. Type-B only calculates the DRTM and relies upon the isolated execution environment provided by DRTM. Type-C provides the security check from BIOS up to dom0 kernel but does not provide DRTM and other security features. Type-D only includes the attestation of VMM and dom0 kernel. Type-E provides no attestation at all.

Third Party (TP)

Third party is introduced for support and to ensure verification of cloud provider. Third party provides trusted service for client on interaction with the cloud provider. It also guarantees integrity verification of the cloud provider as most of the thin-clients use cloud-based services these days. The two main processes on the third party side is the registration process and attestation process. Registration process acts as interface on behalf of TP for client and cloud providers. The attestations of the cloud NC are checked by sending integrity check request to attestation process. The attestations are thoroughly checked and verified based on the results. If the result is satisfactory then the NC gets suggested for ranking based on its attestations. After ranking, the NC gets registered into database using registration process using one of the possible types, based on its integrity check results and attestation. Each registration record contains fields such as NC-ID, registration-Id, endorsement key and NC registration type or rank of the NC.

Each TPM has an endorsement key and it has both public and private portion of the key. Public portion of the is available to open. The private portion of the key is hidden and can't be revealed or accessed out of TPM.

PROTOCOLS FOR TRUSTED EXECUTION FRAMEWORK

Registration Protocol

The node must get registered with the third party (TP) in order to be trusted by it. In step-1 of the protocol, Node Controller (NC) sends request to the TP for registration. The request contains the NC id NC-ID, nonce nNC, public key of NC pubNC which enables TP confidential connection with NC, certificate of NC public key pubNC-certi, the TPM AIK public key of NC pubAIK−NC and certificate of the TPM- AIK public key with all encrypted using public key of TP.

In step-2, TP responds to NC with nonce of TP nTP, certificate of AIK-TP. The certi☐cate of the TP AIK is used to convince the NC that it is indeed the AIK of the TPM of the TP. PCR and its corresponding measurement modules list MMTP is encrypted with TP private key of AIK which represents TP's TPM PCRs. In step-3, NC responds to TP with its attestations and public endorsement key. The response contains nonce of TP along with PCR state and measurement modules encrypted with private key of AIK-NC, public endorsement key. The NC public endorsement key represent secured TPM key that can be accessed only inside the TPM when the PCR state gets matched. The discussed steps are shown in Figure 4.

After receiving response from NC, registration process of the node starts on the TP side. Inside TP, registration process sends PCR and measurement modules (MM) to attestation process for verification of NC platform specifications. As MM contains required modules and their respective SHA-1 hash digests of NC platform. PCR hold various hash digests which are TPM certified. In attestation process, it

Figure 4. Registration protocol

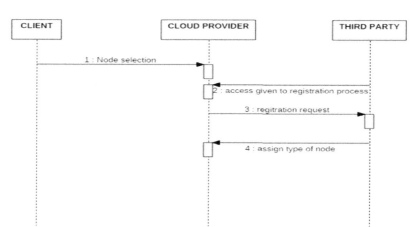

checks the MM values in the hash database of TP. The response is sent to registration process. If the result is satisfactory, it allows the NC for registration. The policy check suggests type of NC to register in database. Now, registration process sends the type to database for registration. In database, each NC is registered with its corresponding NC-ID, NC endorsement key, NC type and its registration number. TP responds the registration type to NC(Khan, I et.al., 2018).

Launching Protocol

After registering the NC in TP, launching protocol is used which in turn provides secure execution of client VM on cloud provider's platform. In step-1, client request cloud provider for VM launch. The VMs are stored in cloud storage and only trusted NCs can access them. On receiving request from client, cloud provides chance to select the NC type in step-2. In step-3, client sends the VM decryption key DVM and client security policy to TP. This policy contains the configuration for NC to meet in order to access the decryption key.

In step-4, TP checks the policy with the policy engine of TP and NC details from DB. After checking, if the results are satisfactory it assigns the Nc type based on the client VM requirement. In step-5, TP sends the decryption key to NC with NC public endorsement key. In step-6, NC reads VM from cloud storage after decrypting with DKVM. In step-7, client connects to VM. These steps are illustrated in Figure 5 (Khan, I et.al., 2018) and (Gunasekhar, T., & Rao, K. T. 2017).

Figure 5. Launching protocol

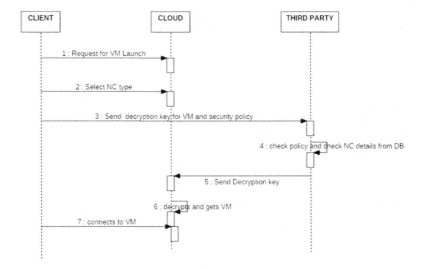

SUMMARY

This chapter introduces various ideas to deal with insider attacks using the research directions, which are discussed in earlier chapters. Here, we mainly concentrated on trusted computing paradigm to enable cloud service provider to solve the potential insider attacks at cloud premises. Trusted computing in cloud ensure the trust among the consumer and cloud service provider to enrich the relation with stakeholders.

REFERENCES

Gunasekhar, T., & Rao, K. T. (2017). Framework for Prevention of Insider attacks in Cloud Infrastructure through Hardware Security. *Jour of Adv Research in Dynamical & Control Systems*, 9(4).

Khan, I., Rehman, H. U., Al-Khatib, M. H. F., Anwar, Z., & Alam, M. (2018). A thin client friendly trusted execution framework for infrastructure-as-a-service clouds. *Future Generation Computer Systems*, 89, 239–248. doi:10.1016/j.future.2018.06.038

Chapter 3
A Survey on Insider Attacks in IAAS-Based Cloud

ABSTRACT

This chapter provides a literature review and the related work about the insider attacks and solutions in cloud environment. The authors classified solutions into three categories: trusted computing-based approaches, encryption-based approaches, and virtualization-based approaches. The trusted computing approaches use remote attestation, sealed storage, and integrity measurement. Encryption-based approaches use the cryptographic operations along with cloud computing security mechanisms and policies. Virtualization-based approaches use the virtualization technology to solve critical security issues using trusted computing approaches. At the end of this chapter, they compare various solutions and summarize the problems and solutions.

INSIDER ATTACK IN CLOUD COMPUTING

According to the cert definition of insider threat "a malicious insider threat to an organization is a current or former employee, contractor, or other business partner who has or had authorized access to an organization's network, system, or data and intentionally exceeded or misused that access in a manner that negatively affected the confidentiality, integrity, or availability of the organization's information or information systems." (Kandias, M., et.al., 2011). an insider attack can be defined as an intentional misuse of computer system which has potential data about an organization. According to this definition attacker can be employee, contractor and/or third party business partners. The damages of insider threat are: it sabotages theft of confidential information, trade secrets and intellectual property (IP). 85%

DOI: 10.4018/978-1-5225-7924-3.ch003

of reported fraud is committed by people within the organization (Kandias, M., et.al., 2011). A typical organization loses approximately 5% of its annual revenue to insider fraud and 330 cases of insider fraud identified during 2010.such that every organization needs secure management of sensitive data and intellectual property. in cloud environment, most of insider threat can be done by cloud insiders such that they should provide robust security algorithm on client data (Theoharidou, M., et.al., 2005).

The Insider Attack

The organizations or cloud providers can recruit participants by word of mouth and advertisements, then participants were can be assigned with terms and conditions. Each condition describes the scenario of the same task to be complete but they provide role that manipulate their "intent" (Gunasekhar, T, et.al., 2014).

Types of Insider Threat

Based on the levels of access privileges, the insider threat can be broadly categorized in to four types:

1. Pure insider
2. Insider associate
3. Insider affiliate
4. Outside affiliate

Each has its own level of access credentials and with different motives, those are described in below sections.

Pure Insider (Employee)

An employee has all access rights and typically they can have badge or keys to their organization data centers. in fact, the employees might well about logical and physical structure of sensitive data because they have every right to access data and company cannot restrict the employees during work hours. so, employees are most danger about to insider threats and the insider threats are possibly by employees of that company only. the elevated insider is an insider who as auxiliary privileges from normal employees. The system administrators or root administrators, who have full power on central data, these kinds of employees may have additional access to do their job but in some cases, they will get more access than they required. in most often to reduce the insider threats, the companies need to strict the people by providing the limited and accurate access to information systems.

The pure insiders can be restricted to insider attacks via three key aspects. One that with limited access privileges that should affect on their general duties (Page, E. C. 1999) and (Gunasekhar, T. et.al, 2015). by doing so we can prevent and easily detect the insider who made malicious activities over sensitive information. Here, the key is controlling and limited access. Second key is fall under the behavior of insiders. In general, someone committed to insider attacks, their behavior pattern might be different from as usual. Such persons openly speak badly about company and/or resources those are assigned to them. They usually very angry about organization and unhappy about workloads and, they are ready to leave the company. The third factor of the pure insiders is money. The general employees could not commit to insider attacks, if the workload and financial problems getting as issue they might be tempted to do attacks. if someone offers lump sum to employees to make all the problems away from them, they might commit to perform insider attacks (Rajan, R. G. 1992).

Insider Associate

Insider associates are not employees, but they have some sort of access in terms of physical instead of network of company. The insider associate might have limited access to physical elements instead of company network. Security guards, cleaners and contractor and/or business partners are fit under this category of employees (Sarkar, K. R. 2010) and (Gunasekhar .T., et.al., 2015 March). After working hours some of the employees may leave their sensitive data on their desk, the insider associate may copy that data and made some malicious activity on data. Here, the problem is that a main key was maintained at central location that can be used by anyone to gain access to office place. Some of the insider affiliates sophisticated about computer resources and they made copy of sensitive data. To prevent such type of attacks, the general employees could be aware of these types of attacks. The employees should understand that the people have auxiliary access privileges and they should lock systems and secure sensitive data before they leave the company.

Insider Affiliate

The insider affiliates are not employees like pure insiders and insiders. The pure insiders and insider affiliates has reason to access company resources but insider affiliates do not. The insider affiliate is friend, spouse, and/or third party client of that organization. in some occasions, the friends of employees may visit to them; they can get access using the employee credentials through the remote access.

When they get engaged with some work, the insider affiliates might theft sensitive information from the employee desk.

This is a simple problem but it may lead to insider attacks (Sarkar, K. R. 2010) and (Gunasekhar.T., et.al., 2015 March). If suppose, the spouse wants to use laptop of employee; the employee might give credential to insider affiliate. She can modify, delete or copy the sensitive data from laptop and it leads to insider data loss or threat.

Outside Affiliate

Outside affiliates are not a part of company and they don't have legitimate access to companies' resources. Unprotected wireless network is a best example. The outside attacker may access the network without any access privileges. so, outsiders are free to use and he can do whatever he wants. it is an obvious problem in companies and companies should aware of such type of attacks. the companies should upgrade security policies and procedures. these attacks are easy to identify or detecting some scenario participants may have fallen on hard financial period among them, the malicious employees or participants can accept a new and higher paying job, which is offered by new company or competitor but they want bring the inside information of old organization. all the participants after completed formalities and pre-study questionnaires and then they will receive necessary components with their respective scenario.

The participants play their role on working hours over specified days to complete their tasks. The resources were configured to monitor both network and host based behavior at all the times (Gunasekhar.T., et.al., 2015 March). When the participants completed they should return resources to the research leads. in addition to this normal behavior, the malicious participants more likely to relieve their jobs into data gathering periods i.e., more logoffs and more logons and indirect data access. Malicious participants also avoided by searching for detailed data by accessing project sites and relevant shared data directories.

Insider Attacks at Cloud Service Provider

The insiders in this scenario are: cloud provider and cloud clients, the malicious administrator working for the cloud provider and cloud clients may miss use their privileges to destroy the cloud data (Gunasekhar, T, et.al., 2014). The malicious insiders may theft intellectual property of other employees and use those credentials to destroy or steal the information systems in cloud data centers. The result of these attacks in cloud data centers will vary from data breaches to data steal of the infected systems and data centers. Detecting such an indirect access is challenging task. All common cloud services like PaaS, SaaS and, IaaS are equally likely insider attacks if the insider has privileges to access datacenters and /or cloud management systems. Hence, cloud computing paradigm could be utilized in order to outsource vast parts of the infrastructure instead of specific services, such as web hosting or application hosting (Anderson, J. P. 1980). The following section will demonstrate the generic model view of an insider attacks in cloud era.

SECURITY PRINCIPLES

This first section is used to introduce the basic requirements and design principles a system should respect in order to the protect the information resident within it.

Basic Requirements

This first section is used to introduce the primary requirements and layout concepts a device need to admire a good way to the guard the records resident inside it. When thinking about the security of a system the primary requirements to search for are confidentiality, integrity, and availability. There are numerous definitions for those necessities however we determined to use the definitions set up by means of the National Institute of Standards and Technology (NIST) .

Confidentiality is the requirement that private or exclusive information now not be disclosed to unauthorized individuals. There are numerous eventualities in which it is important to hold statistics comfortable. For example, the incentive behind the first formal work in pc protection became the military need to put into effect the "need-to-know" principle. The requirement of integrity may be subdivided in statistics and gadget integrity. Some authors additionally recall starting place integrity, which is generally known as authentication (Bishop, M. 2004). For the functions of this document we are going to recognition on the first two. Data integrity states that amendment of records and packages need to simplest manifest in a certain and authorized manner. For instance, recollect a where in Alice requests a fund transfer to Bob with a price of a hundred pounds' sterling. If Mallory can compromise the information integrity of such transaction, she ought to manipulate the bank to procedure the switch to her account in preference to Bob's account.

Guaranteeing device integrity method that the device need to perform the anticipated feature in an unaltered fashion, free from unintentional or planned unauthorized manipulation. A well-known example of in advert system failures became while an Ariane five rocket launch system exploded due to a software error just forty seconds after it had initiated its flight. The venture had a $7 billion improvement fee and the destroyed rocket and its cargo were valued at $500 million.

The final requirement is availability. A gadget satisfies the requirement of availability whilst its valid users are capable of get right of entry to the preferred records or resource. If for a few motive the device is unresponsive to its legitimate users, its availability is taken into consideration com- promised. A well-known malicious strive against a device's availability is a denial of service (DoS) attack. This kind of attack is composed in an adversary flooding a system with illegitimate requests.

CRYPTOGRAPHY TECHNIQUES

This section provides basics of the cryptographic and its importance in the cloud environment. The following subsection gives the brief information about the hashing in cloud infrastructure (Liberal Rocha,F.E.,2015). Most of the people using cryptographic hash functions to secure their messages or conversation over the public networks.

Hash Function

The intention of a one-way hash function is to generate a finger print of a block of ·data, e.g., a report or a message. when parties are making communication, events want to verify if the content material of a message has not modified and that it comes from the alleged source, they use a mechanism for message authentication. Hash features are extensively used in message authentication. allow us to do not forget a hash function H, and listing the homes it desires to fulfill for you to be sensible in the technique of achieving message authentication (Liberal Rocha,F.E.,2015).

1. Hash function takes the data block of length, here data block can be variable size
2. Hash function must generate the fixed size block as an output.
3. Hash code must be computationally infeasible to calculate the original data block.
4. The hash function should be practical as well as it must be easy in computation.
5. More importantly, the hash collision resistant when the function generates the hash code of the given input data block.
6. Hash functions should not take computation time than the encryption and it must be computationally collision resistant.

The above hash function properties are required to maintain message authentication. Top three properties are basic functional components of hash function and collision resistance property ensures the computation speed as well as it must be impossible to decrypt and take the original message. The collision resistance property adds the extra functionality to the hash function such that attacker cannot invert the original data block. If the data block is not invertible then this property can assure the data integrity and data confidentiality of the sensitive data block.

The final property of the hash function is weak collision resistant has to assure it must be impossible to get the original data from other alternative data blocks. It should not generate the same hash code for the two different data blocks. If this is achieved, then hash function can achieve final property. The hash code can be simple in computations and generates hash codes to get the finger print of the data block. The hash functions are majorly used to main the data confidentiality and data integrity in the computer system or during the communication among the two parties.

The hash function can generate the hash codes in a manner that by performing the exclusive-or operation on the given input block. The Secure Hash Algorithm(SHA) is most used hash algorithm to ensure the message authentication. The SHA is originally developed in NIST and its hash code length about 512 bits. Most of the cloud providers using the SHA algorithm to check the data integrity of cloud consumers.

TRUSTED COMPUTING BASED APPROACHES

Virtual Machines

A virtual machine is a computer file, typically called an image, which behaves like an actual computer. In other words, creating a computer within a computer. It runs in a window, much like any other program, giving the end user the same experience on a virtual machine as they would have on the host operating system itself. The virtual machine is sandboxed from the rest of the system, meaning that the software inside a virtual machine cannot escape or tamper with the computer itself. This produces an ideal environment for testing other operating systems including beta releases, accessing virus- infected data, creating operating system backups and running software or applications on operating systems for which they were not originally intended.

Multiple virtual machines can run simultaneously on the same physical computer. For servers, the multiple operating systems run side-by-side with a piece of software called a hypervisor to manage them, while desktop computers typically employ one operating system to run the other operating systems within its program windows. Each virtual machine provides its own virtual hardware, including CPUs, memory, hard drives, network interfaces and other devices. The virtual hardware is then mapped to the real hardware on the physical machine which saves costs by reducing the need for physical hardware systems along with the associated maintenance costs that go with it, plus reduces power and cooling demand.

TRUST ZONES

We characterize a trust zone as a blend of system division and identity and access management (IAM) controls. These characterize physical, coherent, or virtual limits on network assets. Cloud TZs can be executed utilizing physical gadgets, for all intents and purposes utilizing a virtual firewall and exchanging applications, or utilizing both physical and virtual machines. IAM frameworks utilize usernames, passwords, and access control records (ACLs), and may utilize dynamic catalog space controllers, Federated Trusts, and multifaceted authentication mechanisms utilizing time- constrained codes or X.509 authentications. IAM servers can likewise utilize equipment data to settle on getting to choices. For instance, gadgets without a pre-approved MAC address can be kept from joining a system. Switches utilizing ACLs and IP address white listing can keep an unapproved gadget from getting to the network resources. These are cases of equipment based TZ enforcement.

The security of TZ implementations depend on correctly configuring domain controllers, firewalls, routers, and switches that are used in segmenting and restricting access to portions of the cloud network and on "locking down" secure communications between users and domain controllers.

CLOUD ARCHITECTURES

This work is restricted to one cloud deployment model, the Infrastructure as a Service (IaaS) cloud. The layers of the product stack beneath the Guest OS are under the control of the IaaS CSP: the virtual machine administrator (VMM), HV, computing, and storage hardware, and the CCS network. Just the guest OS that structures the establishment of VMs is accepted under the control of cloud inhabitants. IaaS cloud occupants give their own applications and data. The Guest OS might be indicated by the CSP policy, or control of the guest OS arrangement might be shared between the CSP and cloud inhabitant. Due to the common control of the IaaS cloud programming stack, the security profile and status of the CCS relies upon both CSP and occupants.

More vigorous security controls are shaded. Each of the four models utilizes an SDN for tenant VM networking. The first has an insignificant arrangement of security controls. The second join extra data centre physical access, CSP sys-administrator confirmation (authentication), and server equipment port controls. The third designin corporate the security controls of the second one and applies these security controls to all Agency sys-administrator and standard clients. The fourth design incorporates extra cloud architecture solidifying measures.

It has turned out to be progressively mainstream to discuss "cloud computing" as the following foundation for hosting data and deploying software and services. Notwithstanding the plenty of specialized methodologies related to the term, cloud computing is likewise used to allude to another plan of action in which centre registering and programming abilities are outsourced on request to shared outsider foundation, also known as Third-Party Infrastructure. While this model, exemplified by Amazon's Elastic Compute Cloud (EC2), Microsoft's Azure Service Platform and Rackspace's Mosso give numerous points of interest—including economies of scale, dynamic provisioning, and low capital consumptions—it likewise presents a scope of new dangers. Outsider mists empower associations to centre around their core business as opposed to consuming assets on computer foundation and support. The adaptability and versatility of these third-party CCSs can offer critical advantages to government and private industry. In any case, it can be hard to progress heritage programming to the cloud. Concerns have likewise been raised with respect to whether cloud clients can trust CSPs to ensure cloud inhabitant information and whether the CCSs can avoid unapproved divulgence of delicate or private data.

Some of these dangers are plainly obvious and relate to the new trust connection amongst clients and cloud suppliers. For instance, clients must trust their cloud suppliers to regard the security of their information and the integrity of their calculations. Be that as it may, Virtualization, the reason for most CCSs and which empowers CSPs to begin, stop, move and restart processing workloads on interest for augmenting the proficiency, can likewise present non-evident dangers from different clients because of the nuances of how physical assets can be straightforwardly shared between virtual machines (VMs). To expand proficiency numerous VMs might be at the same time allocated to execute on the same physical server. In addition, numerous cloud suppliers permit "multitenancy"—multiplexing the virtual machines of disjoint clients upon the same physical equipment. Hence, it is possible that a client's VM could be doled out to an indistinguishable physical server from their foe. The security status of a CCS relies upon numerous components, including security applications running on the framework, the hypervisor (HV) and related insurance measures, the outline designs used to disconnect the control plane from cloud inhabitants, the level of assurance gave by the CSP to cloud occupant client information and VM pictures, and in addition different variables.

These worries bring up numerous major issues. The government has issued security controls that CSPs must execute to acquire FEDRAMP CCS security accreditation that depends on National Institute of Standards and Technology (NIST) cloud security rules. Be that as it may, these don't furnish high-level decision-makers with a general appraisal of CCS security status or the level of privacy and trustworthiness offered by cloud designs, particularly, those under IaaS. Infrastructure as a Service (IaaS), where central and dedicated resources are shared with contracted clients only at pay-per-use charge to minimize huge initial cost of establishing the cloud which saves a lot money from installing separate servers, networking devices and processing power. Here the basic advantage is to add or remove any application with ease and in a cost-effective manner.

The primary commitments of this report are to dissect diverse structures utilizing Cloud Trust, a cloud security appraisal demonstrate that gives quantitative high-level security evaluations of IaaS CCSs and CSPs and contrast the outcomes and the genuine execution of the cloud design. Cloud Trust gives exceptionally basic and theoretical outcomes that can even be comprehended by cloud occupants so they can make choices in which CSP or CCS gives a superior security to their information. Cloud Trust furnishes you with two probabilities. One, Probability an APT can get to high value (Gold) information and two, Probability the APT is identified by cloud inhabitant or CCS security observing frameworks. Basing on these outcomes we will proclaim the security level of a cloud engineering.

VM Side Channel Attack

This attack is based on VM vulnerabilities identified by (Ristenpart, 2009). It is representative of a class of attacks that take advantage of VM co-residency, which arises when VMs of two or more users share the same hardware. If the attacker's VM is co-resident with the target VM it may be able to glean information from the target VM by observing the hardware's behavior.

SDN Attack

This attack exploits potential vulnerabilities in SDNs. Virtual switches are special purpose VMs that may be co-resident with guest VMs on the same HV. Other configurations are possible including one where the virtue switch logic and code are integrated with the HV. First, the APT gains access to VMs in a cloud TZ (e.g., TZ B) that are logical and network "peers" to the target VMs. This can be done through legitimate means if the only barrier to obtaining a CSP account is payment.

VM Attack Through HV

This attack begins similarly as the SDN assault above. The APT acquires legitimate government client credentials (through spear fishing, observation, or utilization of malware) that can be utilized to get to a VM working in the organization's TZ in the cloud. A related attack way exists in general society cloud. At that point, the assailant acquires an open cloud record and starts VMs in TZ B with the goal of trading off the HV and getting co-residency with an objective organization VM running in TZ A or TZ G. HV compromise continues as in the SDN assault. The APT introduces malware that exploits vulnerability in the HV that empowers benefit level heightening. Once the HV is traded off, the APT gathers information from the host machine's RAM, for example, extra certifications, organized design, and decoding keys to bargain extra VMs and physical machines as fundamental. This information is utilized to find target VMs and to acquire co-residency.

Live VM Attack

In this attack we assume each VM has at least one "local" active administrator account. For this is a local username password account the VM doesn't seek network validation of the logon. The hashed user name and password—that is targeted by the APT. We also assume all VMs in agency TZ have the same local sys-admin logon accounts. The success of this attack and variations on it are dependent primarily on the agency's configuration of its VMs. The attacker illicitly obtains agency credentials from outside the cloud to gain regular user access to a VM in the Agency's TZ A. With these credentials, the APT gains regular user access to an agency VM in TZ A. Depending on the tenant's security configuration, the APT may need to work around additional hurdles such as IP address white listing.

Corrupting VM Images

In this attack VM images are compromised and used to gain access to agency Golddata. We assume agency reference VM images are stored in the cloud. The success of this attack is dependent on the VM image storage controls used by the CSP and agency. For this attack to be effective VM images would not be encrypted, no file access monitoring used and only single factor authentication would be available to tenants.

Disk Injection to Live VM

The attacker attempts to gain access to agency Gold data by placing malicious code in the local attached storage of the targeted VM. Necessary pre-conditions for this attack are that the VM in TZ Gold is operating on a physical machine that hosts VMs in other TZs, and the attacker can conduct network surveillance inside the cloud. The APT can then attempt co-residency with the target. Using similar surveillance, pivoting, and compromise steps associated with earlier attacks, the APT gains access to a VM that is co- resident with a target VM operated by the Agency in its gold

TZ. In this attack, after the APT logons to a VM co-resident with the target VM, the APT exploits vulnerability in the HV to compromise it.

VM Migration Attack

VMs are migrated or moved frequently in clouds to prevent the overheating of servers and to optimally allocate workloads to available physical machines and resources. During workload migration VM memory pages including the OS are copied and moved to a new location. This attack takes advantage of the exposure of a VM during VM migration operations in the cloud.

Through spear fishing and surveillance, the APT obtains user credentials for a VM operating in cloud tenant B TZ.

CSP Personnel With Physical Access

CSP personnel with physical access to the CSP data centre can breach security controls by direct access to physical machines. However, the large number of machines complicates the task. Precision requires the attacker first identify the hardware hosting the target data. The CSP insider cannot make physical contact with every machine in the data centre, but he has several methods to locate the machine hosting the agency TZ G VMs. The first is to enumerate the entire Agency's live VMs. CSP management servers hold such data. A CSP sys-admin will have access to this data.

VMM Control Compromise

CSP sys-admins use VMM capabilities to migrate live VMs, to allow for hardware servicing without execution interruption, or to debug faults using core dumps and memory page snapshots. An attacker can repurpose VMM utilities to compromise agency data.

VMMs can be a privileged VM that runs on top of the HV. The VMM has access to ring 0 privileges and can see other VM's memory and configuration values. If the attacker gains direct access to the VMM, or can corrupt the VMM control channel, they would gain a great deal of maneuverability within cloud infrastructure. Compromising the VMM or VMM control provides the attacker with a path to Agency Gold data by making keys and other sensitive data in an Agency VM visible to the attacker.

Corrupting VM Images2

VM images and instances are vulnerable to attacks from the time they are created, during their transfer to the CSP, in storage in the cloud, while running, and when they are migrated within the cloud. Any unauthorized access or manipulation of VM image file can undermine trust in it.

Infecting images can be more damaging than 'stealing' them because instances based on the infected image will continue to process sensitive data and may expose it to further exploitation. Integrity checks that are both stringent and regularly performed can provide some assurance regarding the health of the image, but such checks can be defeated.

Undetected Configuration Modification

Confining activity to a solitary white listed IP address related to an office enclave is a typical benchmark security control-best practice for restricting access to assets provisioned in the cloud. This, in principle, limits access to the cloud assets to activity radiating from the office enclave, however it doesn't expand all organization enclave insurances and checking to office assets in the cloud (for instance, an IDS might be truant in the cloud, and the CSP SIEM may not get information from fire wall sensuring Agency TZs). Accordingly, the office has less situational mindfulness regarding action on its cloud-based assets than it does inside its enclave. This may enable the assailant to get access to delicate information in the cloud.

Nested Virtualization

A nested virtualization attack utilizes an extra unapproved HV to get too delicate information and certifications. The extra HV could be embedded either between the ordinary HV and the physical equipment or between a guest OS and the typical HV. In the previous case, the extra HV will give an assault surface that traverses all the VMs on the first HV. In the last case, the extra HV could be kept to a guest OS. The objective of the attack is a VM running in TZ G or is a VM image with putting away TZ G qualifications that are at rest.

(Vaquero, L. M., et al. 2011). analyzed the security risks that multi tenancy induces to the most established clouds, Infrastructure as a service clouds, and review the literature available to present the most relevant threats, state of the art of solutions that address some of the associated risks.

(hang, Y. et al, 2012, October), showed that multiplexing approach can also introduce new vulnerabilities. Using the Amazon EC2 service as a case study, they showed that it is possible to map the internal cloud infrastructure, identify where a target VM is likely to reside, and then instantiate new VMs until one is placed co-resident with the target. We explore how such placement can then be used to mount cross-VM side-channel attacks to extract information from a target VM on the same machine.

(hang, Y. et al, 2012, October), they talk about different APT attacks that happened and how they can happen again. APT basic components, how they are dangerous and how one should implement careful measures to prevent these kinds of attacks. Khan et al. proposed a technique to achieve the client data computation confidentiality and integrity in IaaS cloud. The concept of this technique works on Trusted Virtual Machine Monitor (TVMM) and remote attestation, in which trusted party attestation the platform using PCR hash value. The cloud service provider register and attests the NC with remote trusted party using TPM remote attestation property. Such that, trusted party used to establish a trust among cloud client and cloud provider.

(Khan et al. 2011), proposed a technique to achieve the client data computation confidentiality and integrity in IaaS cloud. The concept of this technique works on Trusted Virtual Machine Monitor (TVMM) and remote attestation, in which trusted party attestation the platform using PCR hash value. The cloud service provider register and attests the NC with remote trusted party using TPM remote attestation property. Such that, trusted party used to establish a trust among cloud client and cloud provider.

Zhang, F et.al.,2011, proposed Cloudvisor, it prevents the administrative domain from encroaching data confidentiality and integrity of CC VMs using nested virtualization concept. In Xen based architecture, domain administrator (Dom0) responsible for client VMs integrity and confidentiality. All privileged operations are taken care by both nested and bare metal hypervisor that slowdowns the client applications and I/O interfaces. Thus, nested virtualization concept leads to huge overheads in cloud infrastructure.

Krautheim, F. et.al., (2010, June). analyzed virtual environment on a cloud infrastructure to ensure assurance on data computation and client data. TVEM supports an Intel Trusted eXecution Environment (TXT) and virtualization technology that enables the direct O/I access. In the TXT, designated tasks are assigned to service provider and information owner in this proposed method. TVEM provides ability to information owner to attest the virtual environment for confidentiality and integrity.

Terra proposed by (Garfinkel et al.2003), provides an isolated execution environment in closed box and it is a general-purpose system side by side in a single platform. Terra makes the communication as transparent in node communication with distributed environment using TVMM. The TVMM ensures ability to management VM for resource provision and allocation of storage. TVMM allows remote parties to attest the client VM in closed box execution environment to ensure platform and data integrity and confidentiality. This method prevents administrators and ring 0 privileged users from modifying or accessing client VMs using isolated execution environment that ensures data integrity and confidentiality.

An approach proposed by (Dewan et al. 2008) provides a guard to the sensitive data of client application running in a virtual execution environment. In this approach, client VM may consists malware that may affects the cloud platform. Lightweight hypervisor used in this approach that ensures run time fine grained software memory protection and it places application sensitive data in the specified protected memory location. Then, it registers with client application and accessing of protected memory location controlled by hypervisor or VMM using authentication. This approach provides a locker component to hypervisor or VMM to protect or prevent data leakage from application storage to root kits and malware.

Self-Service Clouds (Butt, S., et al, 2012), restricts the ring 0 privileged administrative domain in Xen environment from examine the client VM contents and computation data.SSC separates the privileged administrative domain tasks into system-wide domain and a per- client administrative domain. Based on the reserved rights, client can perform operation on their own VMs.

Murray et al. 2008, proposed a disaggregation property that makes remote attestation more meaningful and reduce the TCB size. Authors analyzed Xen architecture and they proposed modification in Xen based architecture in the proposed technique. The domain building process moved from administrative domain to special domain called Domain B.

ENCRYPTION BASED APPROACHES

D. Port et al. 2008, protects client application code and data from the vulnerable untrusted legacy operating system using encryption of memory pages of client data and application. The proposed technique called *shim*, allows protected application to run within the VM to interact directly with Virtual Machine Monitor (VMM). The communication among shim and VMM is direct, such that it allows VM to protect its resources. This approach does not consider about an attacker in cloud environment, where attacker may have control over cloud platform and they are potentially powerful in addition with OS.

Tysowski et al. 2013, proposed a protocol that provides access control and data confidentiality in cloud infrastructure. The proposed approach modifies the attribute based encryption to control data access based on certain attributes specified by authorized user of cloud infrastructure. The data owners can find the attributes those are required for data access to protect the confidentiality of data from unprivileged user. Finally, the data owner encrypts and then store data to the cloud to be accessed by privileged users.

A homomorphic encryption scheme (Naehrig, M, et.al, 2011), used by (Lei et al. 2013) to perform sensitive data computation inside the untrusted cloud infrastructure that provides data integrity and confidentiality. The proposed system uses the Matrix Inversion Computation (MIC) that can securely outsource the data to untrusted cloud infrastructure. The plaintext matrix initially encrypted before upload to the untrusted cloud infrastructure. Matrix transformation performed on encrypted data to get the accurate inversion of plaintext matrix. This scheme generates heavy overheads to client and is not adequate for thin clients cloud environments. Our proposed protocol mainly focuses on client data integrity and confidentiality against the insiders such as cloud administrators and employees. The data computations and application execution happens completely in an isolated environment even on the compromised hypervisors. The data computations and sealing are performed at client side, which greatly supports the thin clients.

PUBLIC KEY CRYPTOGRAPHY

This section provides information about the primitive cryptographic concepts and virtualization methods, those are useful in the following sections. The public key cryptographic algorithm invented by diffie and Hellman with the revolutionary concept. The symmetric key cryptographic algorithms depend on the relying on operations over bit patterns but the public key cryptographic algorithms use mathematical operations. Most interesting in public key cryptographic algorithm, which uses two distinct key for operations called "asymmetric" key cryptography whereas in symmetric key cryptography same key used for both encryption and decryption (Kohnfelder, L. M. 1978).

Let us assume about the scenario were attacker trying to break the security of cryptographic algorithm to obtain the encrypted information and every detail of encryption and decryption methods (Kerckhoffs, A. 1883), and (Rivest, R. L et al, 1978). Therefore, an important factor in the security of any cryptographic algorithm depends on computation time to break the cipher and size of the key. In cryptosystems two keys are used such as public key(Pk) and Private Key(pk). Both the keys are created by data owner before performing computation on plaintext data. The public key is distributed to all the groups for later computation whereas private key is always secret and should be secure from attacker stealing's. The public keys can be obtained from the working directories; those are kept for the external entities to make cryptographic algorithms possible. In Stallings, W. (2010b) and Diffie, W. and Hellman, M. (2006)., proposed set of requirements to perform the public key cryptographic algorithms. The list of required elements is enumerated below:

1. **Key Pair:** Public key and private key generation must be easy for bob and alice. For example, Bob keys are Pkbob and pkbob

2. Computations must be easy to generate the Cipher C of message M with public key of Bob: C=encryption(Pkbob,M)
3. Alice should obtain the Message M from Cipher C using Alice private key(pkbob):

M= D (pkbob, C)=D[pkbob, encryption(Pkbob,M)].

4. It should be infeasible to Mallory to compute the private key using public key.
5. Pair of public and private keys used for encryption, must be used for the decryption of original text: M=D [pkbob, encryption(Pkbob,M)]

Three major operations of cryptographic algorithms are encryption and decryption, key exchange and digital signatures. These services are supported with RSA algorithm (RSA Laboratories, 2002). An encryption and decryption operations are similar in both symmetric and asymmetric cryptographic algorithms. In the symmetric algorithm, single key is used for both operations where as in asymmetric algorithm secret key must be shared among the communicating parties to achieve this operation.

Let us assume that Alice and bob want to share some private message with each other. To establish the secure communication among parties, they have generated private and public keys and register public key with the public directory. Set of steps in communication described as follows:

1. Alice visits the public key repository for obtaining the copy of Bob's public key(Pkbob) and hold that key in ring for the future communication.
2. Now, Alice sends the Message M to Bob by using Pkbob. To obtain the original message from cipher C, Bob have decrypt C using own private key.
3. Bob can use obtained message from the Decryption operation. Such that, Bob can only perform decryption on cipher C because Alice used Bob's public key while encrypting the original data.

The above steps illustrate how a secure communication performed among alice and bob using public key cryptography. Here, alice only need to obtain the public key of bob
to encrypt the sensitive information. The public key cryptography only compromised if Mallory obtained or guess the private key using public key. An old public-private key ring can be replaced with the new public-private key ring and update public key in the public key directory for secure communications with other external parties. The creation and management of public-private keys posing challenging to the public key cryptography systems. Digital signature is another service which ensures an integrity and confidentiality among the communication

parties and provide an assurance that information received from the trusted party. The digital signature service follows the following steps:

1. Alice needs to obtain private key from the bob, to decrypt the information that alice received from bob using public key of bob.
2. The algorithm requires two asserts: Block of information and private key for signing purpose.
3. Then, alice decrypt the cipher using the bob public key that guarantees, message M came from the legitimate Bob.

Diffe-Hellman is the one in which secure key exchange happens with minimal operations as following: If Alice want send key to Bob, then Alice signs key using her private key, secure key encryption using private key of Bob and forward it to Bob. This algorithm guarantees the enough secure key exchange among Alice and Bob.

VIRTUALIZATION BASED SOLUTIONS

The idea of using a security kernel to enforce computer security has been around since the early 1970s. A security kernel emerges as a possible reference validation mechanism, which is the combination of hardware and software to implement the concept of a reference monitor (Stanley R. Ames Jr, 1981). The concept of a reference monitor states that all references by any program to any other program, data or device are validated against a policy that defines the authorization for each type of reference according to user and/ or program function within a computer system.

From our point of view, exploring the security capabilities of virtualization is no more than using a hypervisor as a reference validation mechanism which imitates a security kernel in commodity systems. To the best of our knowledge, the solutions that follow are the only known ones that exploit the security capabilities of virtualization which could be used to prevent the malicious insider threat. The following are the hypervisors which are developed by several authors.

SecVisor

SecVisor is a minimal code base hypervisor for the operating systems with the main intention of preventing the advanced kernel level rootkits. A kernel level rootkit is a set of tools that maintains the various administrative tasks or kernel level privileges over the compromised operating system. The objectives of the SecVisor design are a reduced external interface to reduce the attack interface, reduce the trusted computing base to permit the formal validation and reducing the kernel modifications for easy porting of commodity operating systems (Seshadri, A. et al, 2007). An execution of virtual machine under the control of virtual machine monitor in the design of SecVisor allows control over the protection of kernel under which is currently executing. This method allows ensuring the kernel code integrity in the SecVisor design as a paramount.

SecVisor virtualizes the commodity operating system to ensure the memory protection of the kernel's memory space. This enables to reduce the attack interface to the kernel memory of the target operating system because it removes the need of the hypercalls to manage the page table of the virtual machine and host operating system. It simplifies the need of the portability of the kernel changes in to interact with the mentioned hypercalls. This is the advantage of the SecVisor design.

To ensure the data integrity of the kernel code, SecVisor hypervisor programmed to refuse the unauthorized code to execution in the given infrastructure. This enables the consumers or users to specify the security sensitive operations those are listed and policies are maintained to take the decisions on the execution of the security components in the given environment. These policies prevent the alteration of the kernel code as well as it prevents from executing the injected code because those are not approved by the user. The SecVisor hypervisor implemented on top of the AMD powered CPU by taking the advantages of Secure Virtual Machine (SVM). The SecVisor is designed to protect the commodity operating systems ported Linux kernel. Such that, SecVisor does not target the cloud computing environment. However, these design principals are valid to develop a trustworthy cloud computing environment with customized hypervisor.

HyperShot

HyperShot is a hypervisor level component intended to get trust commendable virtual machine snapshots. It was executed in an exploration model adaptation of Microsoft's Hyper-V hypervisor. Since HyperShot is a piece of the hypervisor, which executes at a raised benefit level, a vindictive insider with control over the special administration virtual machine can't take control over the memory space provided to HyperShot (Srivastava,A., et.al., 2012).

HyperShot is a hypervisor-level mechanism designed to obtain trustworthy virtual machines snapshots. The objective of this work is to relocating the snapshot feature into the hypervisor, a higher privilege level of execution guarantee and removing the privileged user to reduce the TCB. This work not concerned with the confidentiality threats.

Dom0 Disaggregation

Murray et al. authored one of the first studies to discuss the problems of having a large trusted computing base in a virtualization environment. They propose a "trusted virtualization" solution where the privileged virtual machine is disaggregated to achieve better overall security.

NOVA: A Micro Hypervisor Architecture

The NOVA approach is based on a micro hypervisor architecture instead of the most common monolithic approach used in solutions such as the Xen hypervisor and the Linux Kernel- based Virtual Machine (KVM) (Steinberg, U. and Kauer, B. 2010). The NOVA approach is based on a micro hypervisor architecture instead of the most common monolithic approach used in solutions such as the Xen hypervisor and the Linux Kernel- based Virtual machines (KVM). The main contribution of this work is to reduce the trusted computing base and it is an alternative approach to the virtualization of computational resources. NOVA does not target the malicious insider threat.

sHype Hypervisor

The sHype hypervisor security architecture implements a mandatory access control policy-based reference monitor for the Xen hypervisor. The objective of this architecture is to use formal security policies that control the sharing of resources between virtual machines through the use of a reference monitor. The reference monitor mediates all security-sensitive operations (Sailer, R., et al., 2005). The sHype hypervisor security architecture implements a mandatory access control policy-based reference monitor for the Xen hypervisor. The objective of this work is to use formal security policies that control the sharing of resources between virtual machines using a reference monitor. A malicious administrator can attack this solution because they are responsible for defining the policies that state which security mechanisms should be deployed.

CloudVisor

Cloud Visor is yet another different secure virtualization architecture where a feather weight hypervisor is placed between the virtual machine monitor and the hardware (Zhang, F., et. al., (2011). The virtual machine monitor is deprivileged together with the management virtual machine. The main objective is to have CloudVisor monitor the hardware resources usage of the virtual machine monitor and the VMs. This

Table 1. Virtualization based solutions

Solution	Confidentiality	Integrity	TCB	Cloud	Insider Attack
SecVisor	✓	✓	✓	✗	✗
HyperShot	✗	✓	✗	✓	✗
Dom0Disaggregation	✓	✓	✓	✓	✗
NOVA	✗	✗	✓	✓	✗
sHype	✓	✓	✗	✓	✗
CloudVisor	✓	✓	✓	✓	✓

positioning allows CloudVisor to enforce isolation while at the same time protect, the resources used by each guest VM.

The Table 1 literature tells us that objective of this work is to provide data confidentiality and integrity along with the trusted boot. The CloudVisor deals with the insider attacks in cloud infrastructure but CloudVisor incurs serious performance penalties, in some cases over 22%, when compared with the Xen hypervisor. Such that an effective framework is needed to mitigate and detect the malicious insiders.

CONCLUSION

This chapter provides information about the literature survey that we undergone during the research work. The literature is categorized into three parts: virtualization-based solutions, Trusted Computing based approaches and cryptographic centric solutions. The virtualization-based solutions concentrate on virtual machine contents of the cloud consumer, Trusted computing based solutions concentrates on the hypervisor or virtual machine monitor and cryptography based solutions concentrates on the encryption and decryption techniques of the cloud consumer sensitive data.

REFERENCES

Ames, S. R. Jr. (1981). Security Kernels: A Solution or a problem? *Proceedings of the IEEE Symposium on Security and Privacy.*

Anderson, J. P. (1980). *Computer security threat monitoring and surveillance. Technical Report, James P.* Anderson Company.

Bishop, M. (2004). *Introduction to Computer Security.* Addison-Wesley Professional.

Butt, S., Lagar-Cavilla, H. A., Srivastava, A., & Ganapathy, V. (2012, October). Self-service cloud computing. In *Proceedings of the 2012 ACM conference on Computer and communications security* (pp. 253-264). ACM.

Dewan, P., Durham, D., Khosravi, H., Long, M., & Nagabhushan, G. (2008, April). A hypervisor-based system for protecting software runtime memory and persistent storage. In *Proceedings of the 2008 Spring simulation multiconference* (pp. 828-835). Society for Computer Simulation International.

Diffie, W., & Hellman, M. (2006). New directions in cryptography. *IEEE Transactions on Information Theory*, *22*(6), 644–654. doi:10.1109/TIT.1976.1055638

Garfinkel, T., Pfaff, B., Chow, J., Rosenblum, M., & Boneh, D. (2003, October). Terra: A virtual machine-based platform for trusted computing. *Operating Systems Review*, *37*(5), 193–206. doi:10.1145/1165389.945464

Gunasekhar, T., Rao, K. T., & Basu, M. T. (2015, March). Understanding insider attack problem and scope in cloud. In *Circuit, Power and Computing Technologies (ICCPCT), 2015 International Conference on* (pp. 1-6). IEEE. 10.1109/ICCPCT.2015.7159380

Gunasekhar, T., Rao, K. T., Reddy, V. K., Kiran, P. S., & Rao, B. T. (2015). Mitigation of Insider Attacks through Multi-Cloud. *Iranian Journal of Electrical and Computer Engineering*, *5*(1), 136–141.

Gunasekhar, T., Rao, K. T., Saikiran, P., & Lakshmi, P. S. (2014). *A survey on denial of service attacks*. Academic Press.

Kandias, M., Virvilis, N., & Gritzalis, D. (2011, September). The insider threat in cloud computing. In *International Workshop on Critical Information Infrastructures Security* (pp. 93-103). Springer.

Kerckhoffs, A. (1883). La cryptographie militaire. *Journal des Sciences Militaires*, 161–191.

Khan, I., Rehman, H. U., & Anwar, Z. (2011, July). Design and deployment of a trusted eucalyptus cloud. In *Cloud Computing (CLOUD), 2011 IEEE International Conference on* (pp. 380-387). IEEE. 10.1109/CLOUD.2011.105

Kohnfelder, L. M. (1978). *Towards a practical public-key cryptosystem* (Doctoral dissertation). Massachusetts Institute of Technology.

Krautheim, F. J., Phatak, D. S., & Sherman, A. T. (2010, June). Introducing the trusted virtual environment module: a new mechanism for rooting trust in cloud computing. In *International Conference on Trust and Trustworthy Computing* (pp. 211-227). Springer. 10.1007/978-3-642-13869-0_14

RSA Laboratories. (2002). *PKCS no.1 v2.1: RSA Cryptography Standard*. Author.

Liberal Rocha, F.E. (2015). *Insider threat: Memory confidentiality and integrity in the cloud*. Academic Press.

Murray, D. G., Milos, G., & Hand, S. (2008, March). Improving Xen security through disaggregation. In *Proceedings of the fourth ACM SIGPLAN/SIGOPS international conference on Virtual execution environments* (pp. 151-160). ACM. 10.1145/1346256.1346278

Naehrig, M., Lauter, K., & Vaikuntanathan, V. (2011, October). Can homomorphic encryption be practical? In *Proceedings of the 3rd ACM workshop on Cloud computing security workshop*(pp. 113-124). ACM. 10.1145/2046660.2046682

Page, E. C. (1999). The insider/outsider distinction: An empirical investigation. *British Journal of Politics and International Relations*, *1*(2), 205–214. doi:10.1111/1467-856X.00011

Ports, D. R., & Garfinkel, T. (2008, July). *Towards Application Security on Untrusted Operating Systems*. HotSec.

Rajan, R. G. (1992). Insiders and outsiders: The choice between informed and arm's-length debt. *The Journal of Finance*, *47*(4), 1367–1400. doi:10.1111/j.1540-6261.1992.tb04662.x

Rivest, R. L., Shamir, A., & Adleman, L. (1978). A method for obtaining digital signatures and public-key cryptosystems. *Communications of the ACM*, *21*(2), 120–126. doi:10.1145/359340.359342

Sailer, R., Jaeger, T., Valdez, E., Caceres, R., Perez, R., Berger, S., & Griffin, J. L. (2005). Building a MAC-Based Security Architecture for the Xen Open-Source Hypervisor. In *Proceedings of the 21st Annual Computer Security Applications Conference, ACSAC'05* (pp. 276–285). Washington, DC: IEEE Computer Society. 10.1109/CSAC.2005.13

Sarkar, K. R. (2010). Assessing insider threats to information security using technical, behavioural and organisational measures. *Information Security Technical Report*, *15*(3), 112-133.

Seshadri, A., Luk, M., & Qu, N. (2007). SecVisor: A Tiny Hypervisor to Provide Life time Kernel Code Integrity for Commodity OSes. In *Proceedings of Twenty first ACM SIGOPS Symposium on Operating Systems Principles, SOSP '07* (pp. 335–350). New York: ACM. 10.1145/1294261.1294294

Srivastava, A., Raj, H., & Giffin, J. (2012). Trusted virtual machines snapshots in untrusted cloud infrastructures. In *Proceedings of the 15th international conference on Research in Attacks, Intrusions, and Defenses* (pp. 1–21). Berlin: Springer-Verlag.

Stallings, W. (2010b). *Network Security Essentials: Applications andStandards* (4th ed.). Upper Saddle River, NJ: Prentice Hall Press.

Steinberg, U., & Kauer, B. (2010). NOVA: a micro hypervisor-based secure virtualization architecture. In *Proceedings of the 5th European conference on Computer systems, EuroSys '10* (pp. 209–222). New York: ACM. 10.1145/1755913.1755935

Theoharidou, M., Kokolakis, S., Karyda, M., & Kiountouzis, E. (2005). The insider threat to information systems and the effectiveness of ISO17799. *Computers & Security*, *24*(6), 472–484. doi:10.1016/j.cose.2005.05.002

Vaquero, L. M., Rodero-Merino, L., & Buyya, R. (2011). Dynamically scaling applications in the cloud. *Computer Communication Review*, *41*(1), 45–52. doi:10.1145/1925861.1925869

Zhang, F., Chen, J., Chen, H., & Zang, B. (2011, October). CloudVisor: retrofitting protection of virtual machines in multi-tenant cloud with nested virtualization. In *Proceedings of the Twenty-Third ACM Symposium on Operating Systems Principles* (pp. 203-216). ACM. 10.1145/2043556.2043576

Zhang, F., Chen, J., Chen, H., & Zang, B. (2011). Cloudvisor: retrofitting protection of virtual machines in multi-tenant cloud with nested virtualization. In *Proceedings of the Twenty-Third ACM Symposium on Operating Systems Principles, SOSP '11* (pp. 203–216). New York: ACM. 10.1145/2043556.2043576

Zhang, Y., Juels, A., Reiter, M. K., & Ristenpart, T. (2012, October). Cross-VM side channels and their use to extract private keys. In *Proceedings of the 2012 ACM conference on Computer and communications security* (pp. 305-316). ACM. 10.1145/2382196.2382230

Chapter 4
Security Flaws and Design Issues in Cloud Infrastructure

ABSTRACT

Information security plays a vital role in cloud computing. Sensitive information should be kept in secure mode for providing integrity and confidentiality from insiders and outsiders. An insider is an employee who has legitimate access to cloud resources which are hosted at cloud data center. They can perform malicious activities on consumer sensitive data with or without malicious intent. This security beach is obvious and the provider needs to protect from such attacks. In this chapter, insider attacks are demonstrated with empirical approach to breach consumer-sensitive data. In this chapter, the authors present the threat models where an insider can manipulate user VMs in the node controller of cloud platform. Here, they assume that cloud service provider is malicious and cloud consumer does not have any security constraints to access their cloud assets. The model described two locations in the cloud infrastructure.

SCOPE OF INSIDER ATTACKS

Attacks in the Local Machine

We assume that the legacy OS with malicious insider at cloud platform. Such that, it clearly states that kernel and user mode is not modified. Such that, an insider can compromise VM's, those are running on controller of target cluster. For example, an insider can modify target VM kernel and they can launch VM with malicious intention without any permissions from VM owner (user). It leads to sensitive data

DOI: 10.4018/978-1-5225-7924-3.ch004

breach of cloud storage of other VM and target VM. With reference of this attack pattern, VM's those are running on NC are in great threat from insiders.

Attacks in the Cloud Administrator

The cloud service provider contains ring 0 privileges to access any content of cloud users and physical resources hosted at cloud data center (Berger, S., et al, 2008). To launch insider attack on resources, insider obtains a memory dump of target VM. Initially malicious insider has no idea about credentials stored in dump of VM kernel image. To obtain a password from kernel, an attacker or insider simply devises a method on obtained kernel of VM. The kernel image filtered using *strings* command, it thoroughly checks dump and returns available strings with name of password. Once insider obtains credentials from kernel of VM, the following are expected issues:

- A cloud service provider can access guest OS contents by using their privileges.

With effect of this cloud client might lose their data confidentiality and integrity. As said earlier, cloud service provider can save, restore, reboot, and shutdown any guest operating system.

- In (Bethencourt,J., Sahai,A., and Waters,B. 2007) and (Rocha, F. and Correia, M. 2011) demonstrated various attack scenarios and those pose great threats in cloud computing virtual environment.
- A malicious insider or malicious cloud service provider can change or breach data upon agreed with competitors of the client company. Attackers (insiders) inside the company have great risk to information resources because they are sophisticated about internal structure.
- Malicious insider cannot access the hypervisor but they can access secondary storage and network I/O. With this maliciousness cloud service provider, can perform any task without any permission from owner of Domain or Virtual Machine.

SECURITY DESIGN FLAW IN CURRENT VIRTUAL MACHINE MONITORS

This chapter provides a proof of the research problem that we addressed in this research work. We studied and analyzed the insider attacks in cloud infrastructure.

This chapter provides a complete detail of addressed problem in cloud environment and various design flaws in virtual machine monitors that leverages and violates the integrity and confidentiality rules of client virtual machines.

The addressed research problem is a hypervisor or virtual machine monitor without least privileges. The failure to defend the privileged user or cloud administrator (malicious) access to the sensitive data which is not accessible that holds cryptographic keys resident in memory space of virtual machine monitor (Rocha, F. and Correia, M. 2011).

The proof of concept presented in this chapter consists of attacks performed in the virtual machine monitor from three major providers of Virtual software i.e., Amazon Web Services (AWS), Microsoft azure, etc. We chose to demonstrate the problem with the most commercial solutions such as VMware ESXi and major open source hypervisor Xen and Linux KVM (Fraser, K. et.al, 2004). This section demonstrates problem in multiple hypervisor vendors that argues in favor of a design issues instead of an implementation of fault tolerance in hypervisor or virtual machine monitor.

This chapter organized as follows: We introduce the attack scenario of our research problem. After, we provide brief description bout the attack we use used against the virtual machine and platforms. The virtual machine introspection is used for detail implementation purpose in two sections. The following two subsections provide information about two dedicated software components and attacking nature that applied on virtual machine and virtual machines. The below section provides the insider threat model of the proposed system. It shows the all the possible flaws which is present in the present hypervisors or virtual machine monitor.

THREAT MODEL

The threat model considers the insiders are malicious with their privileged authentication techniques, those are considered in this section. We have certain assumptions regarding the insider threat implementation.

Assume 1: Insider can modify the hypervisor or virtual machine monitor
Assume 2: An insider can rebuild, compile, and execute an arbitrary software within the cloud infrastructure environment.
Assume 3: Hardware components are unmodified and not used in attack.

Threat Implementation

The idea for the insider attacks we took from the cold boot attacks (Rocha, F. and Correia, M. 2011). The cold boot attack illustrates that cryptographic keys are stored in the random-access memory that contains the virtual machine contents up to some amount of time period. This creates a chance of taking virtual machine contents that an attacker can exploit.

To preserve the contents of extracted random access memory, the cold boot simple cooling techniques are applied and those are connected to some forensic analysis. The cryptographic key and sensitive information can be extracted using simple cooling technique of cold boot attack with disk encryption mechanisms. The major hurdle in the cold boot attacks is to have the direct communication or physical access to the system. In the cloud environment, the cloud employees can launch these attacks since they have physical access to the cloud resources.

The virtual machine monitor manages the virtual machines by allowing them to store the sensitive information in the cloud resources. The Figure 1 illustrates the virtualization environment, where multiple virtual machines can run on top of the physical computer. The illustrated figure represents the array of byte sized with the size of M-1. The virtual machine monitor is a virtual machine player, which holds all the rights over the physical random access memory.

An empirical method proposed in this chapter shows that it is possible to launch the attack without physical access to the cloud components. The malicious insider can simple launch an attack taking exploits of the virtual machine monitor, in our case Xen is the hypervisor or virtual machine monitor. This proved that no need to have the physical access to the cloud components, simply they perform the attacks on virtual machine monitor. As we discussed earlier the cloud virtual machine are launched and monitored by the virtual machine monitor. In fact, the random access memory can be shared among the virtual machine, such that attacker directly extracts the memory contents which are assigned to the consumer virtual machine.

To implement this attack scenario, we used Linux operating system along with Xen hypervisor because both are open source software's and it is possible to change and access the internal contents of the physical resources, which are hosted in the cloud server side.

The empirical attack concepts directly bypass the concept of principle of least privilege can undermine the security concepts of the virtual machine physical host. The attacker can launch the attack on virtual machine monitor by exploring the vulnerabilities present in the cloud virtualization environment and these attack scenarios are still issues in the open source software components which are majorly used in cloud computing environment.

RSA Key Structure in Memory

The RSA private key structure reveals the everything which is loaded in the memory components. If the attacker obtains the private key of the cloud consumer virtual

Figure 1. Virtual machine's memory space.

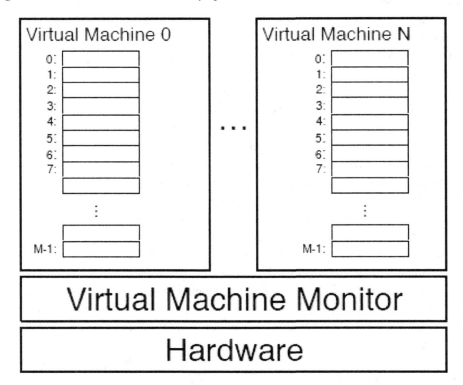

machine, then the attacker can simply uses the RSA private key to take a memory snap of the virtual machine. The RSA key structure is represented in PKCS#12. The representation of the private key in OSI – Abstract Syntax Notation One (ASN.1), which is also represented with four, parts ITU-TX 680 (Heath,N. 2013).This structure specifies the RSA key in the random access memory.

An ISO8824 defines the set of notations and definitions for the values and data types, where as a data value is an instance of respective data type. The set of encoding rules specifies the value of the octets that carry application semantics, referred as transfer syntax. The Figure 2 illustrates the RSA private key ASN.1 in consumer virtual machine dump or snapshot. The ITU-TX.690 (International Telecommunication Union (ITU), 2008b). presents the set of rules includes Canonical Encoding Rules (CER), Basic Encoding Rules (BER), and Distinguished Encoding Rules (DER) for encoding the abstract objects in binary form. The BER consists the CER and DER definitions and differs from each other in a set of boundaries.

The encoding rules are defined in ITU-TX.690 or ISO-8825-1. The encoding should contain the four distinguished components: content octets, length octets,

Figure 2. RSA private key ASN.1 type.

```
RSAPrivateKey ::= SEQUENCE {
    version             Version,
    modulus             INTEGER,    -- n
    publicExponent      INTEGER,    -- e
    privateExponent     INTEGER,    -- d
    prime1              INTEGER,    -- p
    prime2              INTEGER,    -- q
    exponent1           INTEGER,    -- d mod (p-1)
    exponent2           INTEGER,    -- d mod (q-1)
    coefficient         INTEGER,    -- (inverse of q)  mod p
    otherPrimeInfos     OtherPrimeInfos OPTIONAL
}
```

end-of- content octets and identifier octets. These octets must be following this order: identifier octets, content octets, length octets, and end-of-content octets, such that it is a order dependent. The main concentration in our discussion is an identifier octet, which encodes the ASN.1 tag for the different types of data value, set of tags, and is described in (International Telecommunication Union (ITU), 2008b). For instance, an integer value has a tag with a hexa decimal value of 0x02. The identifier block consists of three components such as constructed bit, two-bit classification and primitive type and it is a starting octet of any ASN.1 encoding scheme (Liberal Rocha,F.E.,2015).

The RSA private key is defined as ASN.1 objects identifier available in (Open HUB, 2015), which elaborates the object identifiers for both RSA private and public keys in memory locations. Our primary objective is to extract the private key from consumer virtual machine dump, that we focused in cloud infrastructure to represent the vulnerabilities in the ASN.1 format. The following Figure 3 represents the components of VMI Architecture in the binary representation as per ASN.1 type.

The private key can be searched in the consumer virtual machine dump can be introduced in the cold boot attacks consists of looking to verify the features of DER encoding. As per the cold boot attack pattern no false positive but it happening with our tests to be true. The search algorithm starts to verify the class tag 0x10, but since its encoding must constructed in ASN.1 SEQUENCE type. Then sequence byte chanced to 0x30, and then constructed encoding means the constructed bit in the identifier is active.

The search algorithm finds the RSA version number in the together with the DER encoding tag of next field. The RSA version key is almost zero in all the cases except the cases where multi-prime is used in its DER encoding. The final result from the search is expected octets bytes 0x02 0x01 0x00 0x02, which represent the RSA version of 0x02 is the next type field. Decomposing the RSA version of byte

Figure 3. MI architecture
(Liberal Rocha,F.E.,2015).

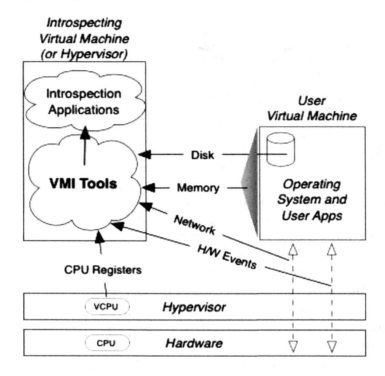

to distinguish the identifier octet of an integer (0x02) that has zero value (0x00) and one byte of length (0x01). We use this search algorithm to locate private RSA keys in memory dumps of virtual machines. More details can be found in the below sections 5.4 with case studies.

CASE STUDIES

This section provides empirical methods that an insider or employee can perform with privileged malicious tasks on consumer data. Demonstrated an attack that damages the confidentiality and integrity of user data in the cloud computing environment. The first attack was easy to perform that takes an advantage of administrator access privileges to obtain the consumers virtual machines snapshot or dump in the cloud environment. We used Xen hypervisor to perform these attacks. The memory dump of the client can be obtained using the single command as root user (Liberal Rocha,F.E.,2015).

Case Study 1

Extracting the Clear Text Passwords

The first attack was shown in (Halderman, J .A,et al., 2009) that extract the clear text passwords from the operating system memory dump in Linux environment. We demonstrate that this attack is possible in cloud environment over the client virtual machines. To launch, this attack the malicious insider issue a command *dump-core,* it is a management command in the Xen user interface (xm or xl). The task of the dump-core command is to prepare the dump memory of targeted virtual machine. A malicious insider has to specify the virtual machines in the dump-core command. After obtain the memory dump, we use cat command to check or verify the password in the dump file and grep is used to locate the password. These commands are listed below, the privileges or password found using theses commands were used for the login into the virtual machines and Apache RSA key that are loginpwd and apachersapwd respectively. Practically, an insider has no idea about the client password those are found in the memory dump. It is possible to automate the password search using TrueCrypt, once an insider obtained a memory dump. In both ways an insider can find the password from the dump in the clear text manner.

```
$ xm dump-core 2 -L sekhardomu.dump Dumping core of domain: 2
...
$ cat sekhardomu.dump | strings | grep loginpwdloginpwdloginpwd
$ cat sekhardomu.dump | strings | grep apachersapwd
apachersapwd
apachersapwd apachersapwd
```

Case Study 2

Obtaining Private Keys Using Memory Snapshots

The primary objective of second attack is to acquire the private key of private- public key pair in the cloud environment. This attack scenario demonstrates how a key obtained from the Apache web server. The key is used for creating or establishing a secure channel with clients. As shown in the earlier attack, the private key is stored in memory dump in the form of plain text format. Here, RSA key is a number either 1024 or 2048 bits.

To launch this attack, a malicious insider obtains a memory dump of client virtual machine, as earlier attack. Now, the insider having keys in the memory dump but memory dump size is minimum of hundreds of megabytes. In this attack, the same technique is used to obtain the private keys from the memory dump as cold boot attack. The cryptographic keys are stored in the memory dump are in recognized format i.e., most using PKCS#1 that represents the keys in ASN.1 object format. Such that, ASN.1 having known structure of RSA key in the memory dump. The *rsakeyfind* tool searches the memory dump to extract the RSA keys in known object structure. The following command shows the attack command sequence on Linux platform.

```
$ xm dump-core 2 -L sekhardomu.dump Dumping core of domain: 2
...
$rsakeyfindsekhardomu.dump found private key at 1b061de8
version = 00 modulus = 00 d0 66 f8 9d e2 be 4a 2b 6d be 9f de
46 db 5a ... publicExponent = 01 00 01
privateExponent = ... prime1 = ...
prime2 = ...
```

With the above mechanisms, an insider can obtain credentials from the consumer virtual machines dump. To implement these methods, we used Xen hypervisor on Ubuntu 13.04 with Linux kernel 3.0.1.

CONCLUSION

This chapter provides information about problem definition of the research work. This section devises an empirical method to prove the vulnerabilities in the existing methods. We addressed and demonstrate possible empirical attacks patterns to strengthen the proposed system. These are performed on virtualization layer of the cloud infrastructure with xen hypervisor as virtual machine monitor and implemented those attacks in the Ubuntu 12.04 LTS 32-bit operating system.

REFERENCES

Berger, S., Cáceres, R., Pendarakis, D., Sailer, R., Valdez, E., Perez, R., ... Srinivasan, D. (2008). TVDc: Managing security in the trusted virtual data center. *SIGOPS Oper. Syst. Rev.*, *42*(1), 40–47. doi:10.1145/1341312.1341321

Bethencourt, J., Sahai, A., & Waters, B. (2007). Ciphertext-policy attribute based encryption. In *Proceedings of the 2007 IEEE Symposium on Security and Privacy, SP '07* (pp. 321–334). Washington, DC: IEEE Computer Society. 10.1109/SP.2007.11

Fraser, K. H. S., Neugebauer, R., Pratt, I., Warfield, A., & Williamson, M. (2004). Safe hardware access with the xen virtual machine monitor. *1st Workshop on Operating System and Architectural Support for the on demand IT Infrastructure(OASIS)*.

Halderman, J. A., Schoen, S. D., Heninger, N., Clarkson, W., Paul, W., Calandrino, J. A., ... Felten, E. W. (2009). Lest we remember: Cold-boot attacks on encryption keys. *Communications of the ACM, 52*(5), 91–98. doi:10.1145/1506409.1506429

Heath, N. (2013). *Linux trailed Windows in patching zero- days in 2012, report says*. ZDNet.

International Telecommunication Union (ITU). (2008b). *X.690: Information technology - ASN.1 encoding rules: Specification of Basic En- coding Rules (BER), Canonical Encoding Rules (CER) and Distinguished Encoding Rules*. DER.

Open, H. U. B. (2015). *Linux Kernel*. Retrieved from http://goo.gl/YYmmyo

Chapter 5
Trustworthy Framework for Insider Attack Prevention and Detection

ABSTRACT

This chapter introduces a trustworthy cloud computing architecture that uses the security properties offered by a virtual machine monitor that enforces the principle of least privilege. These security properties are a strong building block to provide trustworthy cloud computing services to cloud consumers. This chapter briefly explained about a proposed system to prevent insider attacks in cloud environment from cloud consumer and cloud service provider perspectives. The proposed framework is initiating how virtual machines are providing the most reliable security materials of the cloud computing architecture. For cloud consumers, the proposed architecture allocates the well-built security materials of the reliable cloud computing services.

INTRODUCTION

For the reference of the cloud consumers about the cloud computing services to viewed as a how much reliable service they are providing in that case its require to publish the integrity measurement. To reliable the services these integrity measurements can utilize to choose easily for the cloud computing to reliable the services. They should be clearly explained about the security property.

Transparency is a requirement that a remote untrusted system presents integrity measurements to consumers by trustworthy mechanisms. The cloud consumer can easily analyze the system integrity or remote system reliability for these results of

DOI: 10.4018/978-1-5225-7924-3.ch005

the measurement. In this segment, they are defining about the utilization of the reliable virtual machines monitor and computing technology for the cloud computing architecture to build a strong reliability.

METHODOLOGY

This section describes the detailed information about the cloud infrastructure, which is considered for the proposed system. First, Cloud computing server is establishing the security critical software component. Secondly, in clearly they are describing to build a strong reliability cloud computing ecosystem of the architecture requirements. Finally, we discuss how these components and mechanisms come together to create a trusted virtualization environment and give an example scenario where this trusted environment is used to offer trustworthy cloud management operations.

Tradition approaches is different from the components of the cloud server and distinct security related tasks are overseeing for every component. As early we are describing about the virtual machines monitor different for virtual machines are make sure to execute and share requirements of the same physical server is the virtualization layer. The Figure 1 shows the abstract view of the proposed framework. In the proposed architecture, in addition to those tasks, a virtual machine monitor or

Figure 1. Cloud server components
(Liberal Rocha, F.E.,2015)

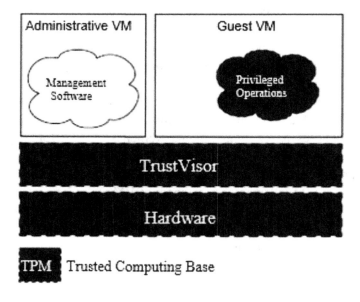

hypervisor (TrustVisor) is also the policy decision and enforcement point for memory access. In security basis, it is very tough about the management virtual machines in previous the whole memory space was assigned to the consumer's virtual machine. In some situations, consumer's virtual machines are directly connected with the hardware requirements it is responsible for the management virtual machines to produce the hardware drivers, virtual storage and network access.

To manage and monitor the virtual machines the present cloud architecture are utilizing the management virtual machines, for the sake of malicious insiders can assess to open in simple way and direct attack vector. In the architecture, we propose in this chapter, however, the privileges of the management virtual machines were reviewed, and the operations that allowed attacks on consumer's data were moved to an isolated special- purpose virtual machine. This isolation implies that the virtual machines monitor must be compromised for an attacker to obtain access to the whole memory range. For consumer's data, they are providing unique requirements for their operations of executing the securit y purposes for example launching and migrating a virtual machine. The cloud service provider should handle these operations very carefully because consumer virtual machines entire memory spaces are engaged to access. These virtual machines can have a reduced trusted computing base if they use solutions such as unikernels, e.g., Mirage OS and OSv. The execution of a single application to accept the development of the kernel.

To implement the single application for growing the kernels at the peak point of the virtual machine, that why we can easily minimize the computing reliability. It could be zero or more controlled by the more request because the consumer virtual machines is the final component. Dumbing down of the management virtual machines is the main distinction of the earlier approaches to minimize the advantage operations. It is main thing to maintain the best security to choose the suitable requirements to the uniqueness of the virtual machine. These servers are required to support trustworthy computing such as Intel's Trusted eXecution Technology (TXT) (Greene, J.(2010)..

A sensitive group NC client maintains TPM enabled hardware support for sensitive information in the cloud infrastructure. In this cloud environment, VM can be size up to 2GB and it poses makes computational overheads while performing encryption and decryption. In general, VM consists of three components: kernel image, boot disk image and an initial ram disk images. From the security perspective, the VM kernel image is most fundamental component of VM and it interacts with the user level application through the system calls. Such that, it is enough to encrypt the kernel instead of entire VM image to maintain confidentiality and integrity of user sensitive data and from the performance perspective.

Our framework uses hardware based security called TPM (Trusted Platform Module), which is proposed by consortium group called Trusted Computing Base

(TCB). The main purpose of TPM is to protect sensitive data from external stealing as well as from internal parties in mobile device, PC and PDA's. In the proposed system, various TPM services are used to secure data of client VM. Our framework works on Infrastructure as a Service (IaaS) model, so we concentrate on VM and its associated assets in cloud environment. As explained earlier, we used eucalyptus cloud software for implementing IaaS based cloud.

Figure 2 briefly shows how proposed system works in cloud. Eucalyptus is open source cloud software and it is API- compatible with EC2.We used eucalyptus design for implementing cloud infrastructure, which is an answer for commercial Amazon EC2. Node Controller (NC) should install on TrustVisor hypervisor and VM's are installing on NC (bare metal hypervisor). To implement the proposed framework, we used open source cloud software called eucalyptus to establish an IaaS private cloud for our testing. Eucalyptus (Nurmi, D., et al, 2009) consists well defined components such as NC, CC, walrus, SC and Cluster Controller (CSC), those provides efficient communication among resources using web- service. Eucalyptus is an EC2 API-compatible and which is an answer to commercial Amazon EC2 cloud infrastructure. Eucalyptus supports libvirt hypervisor, it consists most popular hypervisors Xen and KVM hypervisors. The eucalyptus components are well defined with web-service based interfaces and those components are developed using high-level and standard packages such as Axis2, Apache, and Rampart (Singh, S.,et al., 2016). Our proposed architecture utilizes these components to prove that our concept is secure from insider attacks.

Figure 2. Conceptual view of proposed system

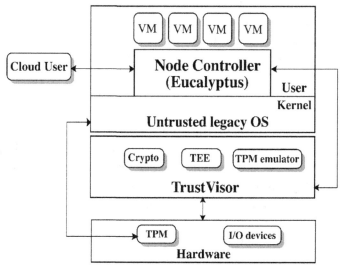

To provide a trustworthy cloud infrastructure, it has some major components and requirements. Here, we provide set of requirements those are considered as paramount for the trustworthy cloud architecture. These requirements considered and addressed from the NIST BIOS integrity measurement (Popović, Krešimir,et al, 2010). These requirements are key to evaluate the trustworthiness of the cloud infrastructure by the cloud consumer. A trusted third party is responsible for generating and maintaining golden integrity measurements of the cloud platform resources.

- Cloud components are capable to generate and collect integrity measurements.
- Trusted Platform Module provides tamper evident or tamper resident storage for integrity measurement.
- A secure protocol must be established to provide a secure communication between cloud consumer and provider to transfer the integrity measurements of the cloud components.
- A protocol must be developed for trustworthiness of software executing in a remote platform.

To satisfy the above requirements, the details are provided in the following sections. The following section elaborates how cloud provider ensures the platform integrity of the cloud infrastructure to assure the trustworthiness of the cloud resources of the cloud ecosystems.

INTEGRITY MEASUREMENTS

The basic requirement for golden integrity measurement is the trusted third party responsible for hosting and managing the genuine software components of the cloud ecosystem, and performs the security tests before collecting and generating the integrity measurements of the cloud infrastructure. A golden integrity measurement can be defined as "it is a cryptographic hash code of the cloud resources which is verified by the trusted third party of the cloud ecosystem to ensure the trustworthiness to the consumer".

The consumer expects this cryptographic hash before using the cloud resources when verifying the trustworthiness of the cloud components such as Virtual Machine Monitor or hypervisor. The proposed framework, golden measurements are intended to offer functionality similar to the one possible using reference integrity metric (RIM) elaborated in the mobile trusted platform specification.

The reason to use the cryptographic hash is that it is impractical to generate same for the other components and cryptographic hash use is a logic layout choice because cryptographic hash capabilities are collision-resistant, this means that it is computationally impracticable to find a distinctive enter that gives the equal output/hash. Therefore, if a certain block of code has a hash h1, it's far impossible to use a different block of code, as input to the cryptographic hash characteristic, and obtain the same hash h1. This belonging is fundamental in assuring that an integrity measurement is explicitly certain to a single block of binary code and/or data. However, a golden integrity measurement does now not have the objective of presenting information on the presence or absence of vulnerable properties, e.g. Buffer overflows, within the measured binary code and/or data.

The proposed framework foresees the generation of golden integrity measurements as a robust addition to the security development lifecycle. The security improvement lifecycle is composed in a hard and fast of traditional software development lifecycle phases with the addition of protection steps that intend to attain a final product as resilient as feasible in opposition to malicious insider attacks or breaches. The levels include necessities, layout, implementation, verification, and launch. The verification segment already calls for an impartial team to perform a final security review of the product [79]. Therefore, it has to be trivial to deliver within the era of valid golden integrity measurements.

Although a secure hash characteristic offers certain security properties, it isn't always sufficient to ensure the authenticity of golden integrity measurements. Let us consider a scenario in which a cloud provider develops his very own infrastructure management software and generates himself the golden integrity measurements. In such cases, if customers agree with the provided golden integrity measurements then they're nonetheless susceptible to attack originating from an insider threat within the cloud provider infrastructure. Hence, we propose using trusted authorities together with the ones within the properly-set up public-key infrastructure (PKI). This technique builds a chain of trust, in which the consumer can believe to verify the authenticity of golden integrity measurements. In what follows, we explain in detail how such chain of trust is executed. The number one intention of imposing a public-key infrastructure is to permit at convenient, secure, and efficient distribution of public keys. A public-key infrastructure (PKI) is defined as the set of physical or logical entities and techniques required to obtain such a goal. The required procedures address the creation, control, storage, distribution, and revocation of digital certificate primarily based on asymmetric cryptography [80].

The general public-key certificates are the important component in a public-key infrastructure due to the fact it is a scalable and secure way for the distribution of public keys. Earlier algorithms depended on a primary public-key authority which would keep each public key and distribute them to cloud consumer using a direct request method. Therefore, it'd constantly be involved in the transactions turning into a single-point of failure and a bottleneck. The digital certificates are exchanged without interference of the certificate authority. Even though it is secure the trusted party is entitled as certificates authority (CA) is required. A certificates authority is commonly a security company, government, or financial organization trusted within the user network.

The generation of a digital certificate is an essential for the consumer to transmit its public key to the certificate authority in a reliable and secure manner. An unsigned certificate is essentially the cloud consumer public key and its information that uniquely identifies the consumer, and certificate authority identification information. The certificates authority makes use of a secure hash feature to achieve a hash code of all this information and encrypts that hash code using its private key to create a digital signature. This signature is then forward to the certificate. The user can then make the certificates public for anyone to apply or transfer it as a respond to consumer requests.

Figure 3 illustrates how the party using the certificate can verify the user's public key through the digital signature attached to it. This signature is verified using the certificate authority's public key to decrypt the signed hash code and comparing it to a hash code the verifying party generates from the certificate data. A match between the hash codes guarantees the user's public key can be trusted. For a more detailed description on the contents of a digital certificate were further readers to the X.509 specification (International Telecommunication Union (ITU) 2008b).

Let us consider as an example the generation of a golden integrity measurement for a specific hypervisor version. During the verification phase of the security development life- cycle an independent and trusted authority would perform security checks on the software. In case those verifications were successful, it would generate a golden integrity measurement for the software and sign it (i.e., encrypt the hash code of the software) using its private key. The public key of this trusted authority can be obtained through its public- key certificate.

It is important to clarify those using golden integrity measurements to offer trustworthy software does not mean only a software version is valid. A version is considered valid as long as the golden integrity measurement in use as a valid signature attached to it. For a cloud consumer to verify the trustworthiness of the hypervisor it just needs to have in his possession the correspondent golden integrity measurement and the trusted authority's public-key certificate.

When communications are initiated with the cloud provider's infrastructure, the consumer receives a fresh signed integrity measurement of the hypervisor in use together with public-key certificate from the cloud provider. For the purpose of this discussion it is enough to know there is a digital certificate linked with the cloud provider, more details about which certificate and why we can trust the provided integrity measurement are given in Stallings, W. (2010a).

The consumer can then check if the received integrity measurement matches the golden integrity measurement. If there is a match, then the consumer can trust the

Figure 3. Public key signing

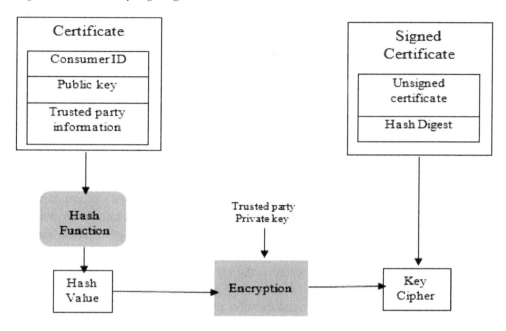

hypervisor version execution in the cloud infrastructure. The public keys of both trusted authority and cloud provider allow the client to verify the authenticity of the measurements used in this verification.

PLATFORM INTEGRITY MEASUREMENTS

This section discusses how our architecture possesses components capable of generating and collecting integrity measurements, and offers tamper resistant or tamper evident storage for integrity measurements. These requirements are satisfied through the support for hardware- based security such as Intel's Trusted Execution Technology (TXT). Therefore, the servers require the presence of a Trusted Platform Module (TPM).

The TPM-chip provides the foundation for hardware-based security, and contains cryptographic functional units (e.g., random number generator), non-volatile, and volatile storage. It is tamper-proof and the hardware root of trust in a trustworthy environment. A root of trust is a hardware or software mechanism that the user implicitly trusts. The definition of trust considered in this document comes from the Trusted Computing Group (TCG): "An entity can be trusted if it always behaves in the expected manner for the intended purpose". The TPM generates, collects, and offers the tamper resistant storage for integrity measurements. However, using the TPM directly to manage integrity measurements has proved to be a scalability and performance issue.

Our approach to address the performance issues related to intensive use of the TPM is combining TPM functionality with a minimal software implementation of the TPM standard denominated micro-TPM. The concept of a micro-TPM was introduced in TrustVisor as a solution to offer fast integrity measurements of pieces of application logic (PAL). For the use of a software-based micro-TPM to be successful it must be combined with the specific functionality from the hardware base TPM. In what follows, we discuss in detail how these two requirements allow for trustworthy management of a platform's integrity measurements.

In this section, the software and components of our proposed system capable of collecting and generating integrity measurement, and offers tamper evident or resistant storage for platform integrity measurements. These properties can be achieved by using AMD's Secure Virtual Machine (SVM) and Intel's Trusted eXecution Technology (TXT). Therefore, the servers require the presence of Trusted Platform Module (TPM).

The TPM-chip provides the foundation for trustworthy, contains cryptographic functional units, volatile and non-volatile storage. The TPM is tamper-proof and provides a root of trust cloud environment. A root of trust is a hardware or software mechanism that the user implicitly trusts the resources, which are hosted in cloud environment. According to the Trusted Computing Group: "It can be anything, which acts or behaves in a intended manner". The TPM can generate, collect and offers the tamper resistance storage with volatile and non-volatile memory. Though it provides durable security for sensitive information, TPM ensures the performance and scalability issues.

Our approach uses the micro-TPM concept to ensure the data integrity and data confidentiality of the consumer virtual machines. The direct impact of the TPM is high and generates less performance while generating and collecting integrity measurements. The micro-TPM was implemented in TrustVisor hypervisor as an alternative to improve performance of computing system while generating integrity measurement of cloud components. The micro-TPM concept generates and collects the integrity measurement of the Piece of Application Logic (PAL). To make this as a possible to implement this with the software based micro-TPM, it must be collaborative with physical hardware of the computing system or cloud server. We can discuss how the requirement allows trustworthy management of the given platform's integrity measurements.

One, the physical TPM has direct impact during the generating and collecting the integrity measurement of hosted components. To overcome this issue, we need to implement the micro-TPM concept to incur the high-performance issues as resulted in Flicker. The software based micro-TPM concept was implemented generates the high performance in hosted primary computing components, while implementing restricted set of functionalities by physical TPM. The micro-TPM implementation should offer the remote attestation, data sealing, randomness and measurements. Every consumer virtual machine will have the micro-TPM to generate and collect the platform's integrity measurements. The TPM property tamper evident can be achieved by using the concept of micro-TPM or physical TPM storage locations. The second property is to ensure the trustworthy computing environment while executing the virtual machine. The trustworthy computing can be achieved by using Static Root of Trust for Measurement (STRM) and Dynamic Root of Trust for Measurement (DRTM). In the initial stages of the trusted environments, the BIOS were used as STRM. The STRM's trusted computing base includes Boot loader, OS, BIOS, applications and ROMS. The STRM ensure the secure execution environment by using the secure boot, where every line in the software involved in the boot sequence is trustworthy. By combining all these components, it creates a large trusted computing base. If the size of the trusted computing base increases, then the possibilities of vulnerabilities also increases.

The recent advancements in the technology, the computer vendors developed new technology to create a trustworthy environment, such as Intel's Trusted eXecution Technology (TXT) and AMD's Secure Virtual Machine (SVM) to ensure the Dynamic Root of Trust for Measurement. These are used during computation to ensure the trust over the hosted components in cloud environment. The second generation of DRTM provides a concept called late launch, where the applications can be executed at any time by generating and collecting platform's integrity measurement. The advent technologies from the major vendors provides the dynamic execution environments by using the Intel's SENTER and AMD's SKINIT instructions that allows to execute the application in the trustworthy execution environment and these instructions can reset. These secure initializing instructions can initialize the CPU, load the Secure Loader Block (SLB) code, sends the SLB contents to the physical TPM, and enables the Direct Memory Access for the SLB and control will be transferred to the SLB. Then the SLB can launch the application from trustworthy state and this process reduces the TCB by eliminating the ROMS, BIOS and Boot loader.

A security sensitive code blocks or piece of application logic should be register for node controller to put in place the appropriate security measures for its execution. This piece of code assures the data confidentiality and integrity of the consumer data and applications in the cloud infrastructure. The execution integrity can be ensured that when application A executes with A inputs, it always returns A outputs. The life cycle of PAL includes registration with node controllers, triggering or invocation, termination, and deletion or removal. Figure 4 demonstrates the three execution

Figure 4. PAL system execution modes
(McCune et al, 2008)

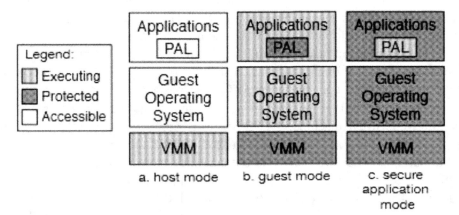

modes of system and how it provides memory protection in each mode. The highest privilege level is granted in host mode when the virtualization layer is executing and has control of the system.

The virtualization layer has full control over the node controller memory, which means it can manipulate guest operating system, memory regions of PAL, and the applications on top of the consumer guest operating system. When the system is in guest mode, the virtualization layer must protect its memory regions as well as memory locations of PAL. The secure application mode is most restrictive mode, when PAL is under the execution. The secure application mode virtualization layer isolates the PAL's memory locations from all the node controller resources.

The registration process of PAL is already secure from the malicious insider attack as illustrated in the proposed framework. However, the security sensitive operations are performed in the special purpose virtual machine and the remaining operations are concern with physical system over which those are executed. The registration can be done by using application level hyper calls from the hosted hypervisor on the node controller of the proposed architecture. This registration process consists of set functional entry points with expected input and output. The virtualization layer is responsible for verifying that the providing entry points to executing application, while ensuring that the node controller or operating system does not perform any malicious tasks to the memory regions of the guest operating system as specified as security sensitive. The security sensitive code components should have the integrity measurement, which allows the cloud consumer to verify the integrity of the cloud resources in cloud infrastructure. The PAL can invoke as if affected application or code is running normally on top of the node controller.

However, after registration the memory locations of the PAL are no longer available to the application and hosted operation system.

The virtualization layer is responsible for handling the security sensitive operations of the PAL, when the PAL is invoked within the applications. When the PAL is invoked, virtualization layer hypothesized the control and setup the environment for execution of PAL as follows: (1) locate the registered PAL to which the executing sensitive code belongs to, (2) change from guest mode to secure application mode so the memory access is restricted to the memory pages of the executing PAL, and (3) prepare the execution environment so control can be passed to the executing PAL.

After finishing PAL's execution, the virtualization system should attain control over the applications hosted in the operating system. When the system is executing in the secure application mode any attempt to execute code those belongs to the PAL memory locations returns control to the virtualization layer.

The virtualization layer process the PAL output results and make them made available to the calling application. The execution mode switched from secure application mode to guest mode, in which PAL memory space is no longer accessible to the guest operating system. An application any can PAL at any time with different input parameters within the guest operating system perimeter. The PAL removal can be originated from the application that requested for the registration.

After removing the PAL, security sensitive list associated memory pages are emptied or zeroed and which is made available to the node controller. This security measures assure data confidentiality and integrity, and code and execution integrity by isolating the execution environment from the host platform. The PAL provides the application isolation and integrity measurements from virtual machines.

CLOUD INFRASTRUCTURE TRUSTWORTHINESS

In this section, we present how the trustworthiness of a cloud platform can be shared with cloud consumers increasing the level of transparency when compared with current approaches. To protect the confidentiality and integrity of data kept in the cloud, the cloud platform has to prevent certain attacks and give consumers the ability to assess that this protection is in place. The latter requirement may seem excessive, but it arises from the concern we are dealing with: the insider threat. A malicious insider is in a sense part of the cloud, so he or she can provide false information to the consumer.

Trusted Virtualization Environment

Our solution for protecting consumers' data (and applications) in the cloud assumes that the attacks against the virtual machine come through the infrastructure and not from targeting vulnerabilities in the consumer VMs themselves (Liberal Rocha,F.E.,2015).

Remote Attestation

The remote attestation is a process of verifying trusted virtualization layer of consumer hosted environments. In the remote attestation, the set of measurements are collect from the resources, which are located at cloud provider side. These measurements are used to represent present state of the cloud resource which are held by cloud consumer. The Dynamic Root Trust Measurement based remote attestation, the consumer receives the integrity measurements of the cloud assets such as hypervisor, those controls the cloud server. The Figure 5 provides an illustration of the remote attestation process, that allows the remote party to verify the platform integrity of the of the cloud resources. The communication must be established the consumer and cloud service provider i.e., cloud server. Let us consider the scenario where the consumer uses the computer without the scope of the security aspects of the cloud security.

The remote attestation process starts from the consumer request. First, the cloud consumer requests the integrity measurement from the cloud server, here the hypervisor send the platform integrity measurement of the hypervisor. Second, the TPM sends the quote operation result to the software agent by receiving the request. Third, the TPM sends the signed platform configuration register that holds the all the integrity measurements of the components that are hosted in the cloud server

Figure 5. Remote attestation

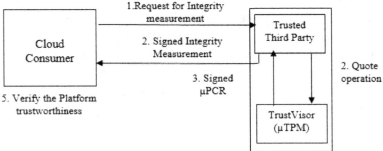

side. The cloud consumer generates the nonce, which is included with the signed values of integrity measurements. Four steps, the message forwarded to the respective consumer that holds the signed integrity measurement. Fifth, the cloud consumer verifies the signature and if the measurements are matches, then the hypervisor is concluded as a trusted component. This remote attestation process allows the cloud consumer to verify the hypervisor on cloud provider platform.

The cloud consumer behavior based on the trusted party with the trusted cloud components by using above five step remote attestation process.

- The result of matching the integrity measurements tells the cloud consumer to trust the components or not.
- An activity of requesting an integrity measurement from the software agent which is located at cloud provider side. The cloud consumer has to trust the software components otherwise they have to notify the provider about the malicious activity of the software component.
- If the integrity measurement is matched with old or stored integrity measurement with malicious activity of the software component at the cloud service provider side then the cloud consumer has to notify about the malicious component and terminate the communication.

The above explanation gives brief information about the traditional remote attestation process, where the physical machine's trusted platform module is used for generating platform integrity measurements. The proposed architecture, the transitive trust must be established among the cloud consumer and cloud components which are hosted at cloud server. Let us assume the scenario, where the cloud consumer agent added the hypervisor to trusted computing base to the cloud environment and micro-TPM can generate and collect integrity measurements for future purpose to verify the components and speedup the verification process. The micro-TPM acts like cache memory during the attestation process of the cloud components. This scenario clearly states that consumer is implicitly trust the cloud components which are hosted at cloud provider side. The remote attestation verification can be performed between the cloud consumer, cloud server and trusted verified. The micro-TPM can collect the integrity measurement of the virtual machine of consumer on hypervisor platform.

Critical Management Operations

This subsection provides information about the virtual machine launch, backup, migration and termination and how these operations are performed to ensure the trustworthy architecture, which is presented (Rocha, F., et al, 2013a). This information doesn't provides the entire critical operations of the cloud architecture, it simply provides the some of the operations with illustration of how proposed architecture provides the more transparency during the protection of the cloud consumer sensitive data. This process and operation allows the cloud consumer to verify the cloud components which are located at cloud server.

The remaining critical operations are protected in the same way. These kinds of operations are also an example of the micro-TPM that measures the software components at cloud provider side. The boot process will load all the components integrity measurements while loading the on top of the hypervisor, these integrity measurements are loaded into the physical TPM of cloud server. These integrity measurements are used establish the initial trust among the major parties in the cloud such as cloud consumer and cloud provider. In this process, the trusted hypervisor plays a major role while collecting the integrity measurements and comparing with old integrity measurements. Then it established the trust among the parties with the help of the trusted third party. The remotely executing hypervisor can establish a trust using the remote attestation process, which presented in the section above and Figure 5. The remotely executing software integrity measurements are passed to the micro-TPM component for the trust over the hosted software components at cloud server.

In this section, we assumed that software communication agent is located at both ends of the communication parties to make remote attestation process more successful and verification of the computing components. The communicating software party is responsible for making the verification at both ends of the cloud consumer and cloud provider side. This process is divided into sub-operations, which are clearly described in this section numerical in word. These steps make the communication even better than the conventional process of remote attestation process.

Virtual Machine Launch

In the proposed architecture, the virtual machine launch operation objective is that the consumer should trust the software components those are hosted at cloud provider side. The virtual machine operations are handled by software agents in cloud environment, where the cloud consumers outsource their sensitive data.

Figure 6 illustrates the overall process of virtual machine launch. First, the process of secure virtual machine launch protocol starts with cloud consumer software communicates with software agent which is resided at cloud server side, which is responsible to manage the all cloud resources in the cloud environment. Second, this interaction implies to mean that to launch the virtual machine within the perimeters of the cloud infrastructure with privileged access levels and consumer can access virtual machine using the given physical address of the cloud provider.

Figure 6. Secure VM launch

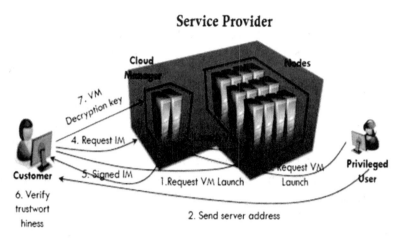

Now it's time to make communication among the cloud consumer and target cloud server. Four, the consumer has to request the integrity measurements of the cloud platform to the cloud server, where the consumer virtual machine is supposed to launch. Fifth, the target cloud platform generates and signs the cloud server's micro-TPM, then sends back to the consumer for the verification purpose of the integrity measurements. Six, the consumer verifies the signature and checks the integrity measurement which is corresponds to the current integrity measurements of the target hypervisor, where the virtual machine is supposed to launch and run.

If the verification is successful, the consumer establishes a secure communication channel with the privileged operations virtual machine and sends the symmetric key necessary to decipher the encrypted virtual machine image (7). An approach for exchanging the key could be using the public portion of an attestation identity key associated with the micro-TPM of the destination server. The virtual machine image can be sent by the consumer or be collected from a local repository (8). Finally, the VM image is deciphered using the key the consumer provided (9) and the process is concluded with the launch of the virtual machine in the cloud server (10). The communications between consumer agent and privileged operations virtual machine software agent are handled in the destination server agent which can be software part of the management software of the server.

This management software is part of the management virtual machine as seen in Figure 1. In step six of Figure 6, the secure communications channel between privileged operations virtual machine can use inter-virtual machine communication solutions to avoid bloating the trusted computing base in the privileged operations VM. The advantages and performance of using such channels to handle communications between virtual machines.

Virtual Machine Migration

From the consumer's perspective, verifying if the initial server (where his virtual machine is instantiated) is trustworthy is not enough because virtual machines can be migrated to different cloud servers within the cloud infrastructure. However, this problem can be easily solved by having the source cloud server verify if the destination server is trustworthy. The consumer has already verified that the initial server is trustworthy, so that guarantees that the virtual machine migration operation can be trusted to perform the steps represented in Figure 7. The communications between the involved servers are handled in the respective management virtual machine. The data can then be sent to the privileged operations virtual machine using inter-virtual machine communication channels in order to keep the trusted computing base to a minimum.

Consider a scenario where an attacker tries to migrate a virtual machine from a trustworthy server to a platform over which he has total control. This attack wouldn't go through because the source server would reject the migration when the integrity measurements do not match a trustworthy virtualization environment. Furthermore, the privileged operations virtual machine should have software agents responsible for logging and auditing these operations to detect any anomalies.

The remote attestation process can be happens between the cloud server and cloud consumer, to check the integrity of the source platform where the cloud server launches the consumer virtual machine. The Figure 7 explains the remote attestation process, the cloud server is placed at remote location. The initial process starts with the cloud server agent sends a migration request. The cloud server sends the remote attestation of target server's platform integrity, then the destination server request for the quote operation from the virtual machine micro-TPM. Next, the signed

Figure 7. VM migration

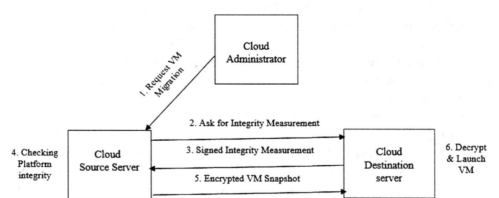

platform integrity of the cloud environment is sent to the requested server. Fourth, the platform integrity and signatures are verification will be happens at trusted party side to decide whether a given platform is trustworthy or not. Fifth, if the verification is successful then the encrypted virtual machine will be sent along with the decryption key to the destination server, where the consumer virtual machine will be launched. Sixth, the destination server decrypts the virtual machine and launches in the verified platform.

Virtual Machine Backup

One of the major attractive characteristic of cloud storage is to provide an environment that might almost possible for successful accomplishment of the on-demand network access. The cloud system scenario will be like consumer stores the data and then access the contents by using the interfacing components. The online storage system must be available to the cloud user until consumer stop receiving services. To ensure the data availability, the cloud provider must maintain a backup service from the cloud components. The backing up consumer information is also presents the some security requirement, which are follows and must be satisfied.

The virtual machine backup process assumes that virtual machine which is launched on cloud server is trustworthy. It can be verified by using the remote attestation process and they will launch if the virtual machine is trustworthy. If the virtual machine is undergoing to the backup server then the virtual machine migration step will takes place before the virtual machine snapshot is backup. The virtual machine backup steps are explained in Figure 8. The virtual machine backup process is very simple

Figure 8. Trusted VM backup

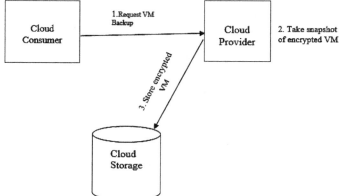

and process of backup is as follows: first, the consumer agent sends an encryption key and VM backup request for cloud service provider or designated cloud server.

Then, then cloud server takes the VM snapshot of the consumer virtual machine and encrypts it with key, which is provided by the consumer. During the virtual machine launch, encrypt with same key to launch the target virtual machine. Finally the encrypted virtual machine will be storage in the designated storage location.

Virtual Machine Termination

The virtual machine termination is simple process and it should be discussed to mitigate the security vulnerabilities in the process. This can be important when the memory space is due during the life cycle of the virtual machine.

Suppose, let us assume that where the application executing in virtual machine persists the private key for the key exchange to sign the values. This clearly states that private key is present in the volatile memory of the virtual machine for signing operation. After termination, the memory space of the virtual machine must be zeroed or randomized, if it is not happening then the attacker creates a special purpose Linux image to corrupt the virtual machine and try to collect the sensitive data from the remainder of the memory.

The virtual machine can be termination process is described and illustrated in the Figure 9. At initial stage, the cloud consumer can request to the cloud server for the virtual machine termination. Then, the consumer can encrypt and store the virtual machine snapshot and it must be located in the cloud infrastructure. The

Figure 9. Virtual machine termination

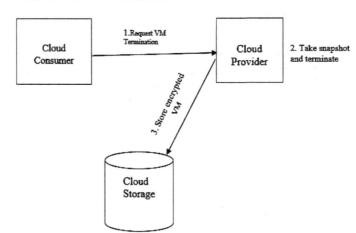

cloud consumer can request to launch the virtual machine and decrypt it with the same symmetric key in the cloud premises.

For maintain the security during termination process, the cloud server must terminate the virtual machine with zeroes or randomizes the memory space and they encrypt the virtual machine snapshot using private symmetric key. Then, the virtual machine will be stored in designated location within the cloud premises. The cloud server make sure about the virtual machine state i.e., whether those locations are zeroes or randomized. If it not randomized, then the termination process must happen to protect the security sensitive information.

IMPLEMENTATION

This section describes the proof-of-concept of our proposed protocol architecture as described in earlier sections. In order to ensure the trust worthiness of cloud platform a remote attestation concept, we used most popular and widely used method called Integrity Measurement Architecture (IMA) (Sailer, R., et al., 2004, August). Remote attestation uses IMA; it works based on binary attestation concept. After configuring IMA, it calculates and extends the hashes of all components while boot process into their respective PCRs. To ensure the remote attestation with privacy preserving of NC, we used Attestation Identity Key (AIK) for signing hashes of PCRs while performing *quote* operation. We used TPM emulator for communication with TPM device using TPM driver.

The NC is the central component of our proposed eucalyptus cloud frame work, where CC can launch and execute VMs. Eucalyptus cloud software installed as NC in HP ML150 server with 1.67GHz Xeon processor and 12GB of RAM or primary memory. Initially, NC running on Ubuntu 12.04 with libvirt hypervisor process. Here, cloud clients are divided into two groups: sensitive group users and normal users.

The NC's are register with the front-end node for user interface. The consumer request NC with public key Pkc and nonce value for VM execution. The NC verifies the public key Pkc and nonce then forwards the public key and nonce (which is received from the consumer) to the TrustVisor module through TPM. TrustVisor verifies the Pkc and then acknowledge with the nonce to consumer for private key pkc. The pkc of consumer provided to TrustVisor for decryption of VM and NC decrypt VM with pkc. Now, consumer can access the VM and every VM consist µTPM for securing the contents by its own. The µTPM is a part of the TrustVisor on NC CPU, such that it eliminates the unfavorable performance impact on frequent usage of dynamic root of trust (vTPM, Flicker (McCune et al., 2012)). The TrustVisor is a bare metal hypervisor, which provides an isolated execution environment and "micro" TPM concept for securing VM contents through Secure Sensitive Code Block

(SSCB). Secure sensitive code blocks are formally known as Piece of Application Logic (PAL). The PAL provides an isolated execution environment by using trusted execution environment technology.

CONCLUSION

In this chapter, the proposed trustworthy architecture provides the data integrity and confidentiality of cloud consumer virtual machines. The proposed framework provides a trust over the cloud resources using secure virtual machines launch and remote attestation protocols.

REFERENCES

McCune, J. M., Parno, B., Perrig, A., & Reiter, M. K. (2008). Flicker: An execution infrastructure for TCB minimization. *Proceedings of the ACM European Conference in Computer Systems (EuroSys)*. 10.1145/1352592.1352625

Nurmi, D., Wolski, R., Grzegorczyk, C., Obertelli, G., Soman, S., Youseff, L., & Zagorodnov, D. (2009, May). The eucalyptus open-source cloud-computing system. In *Cluster Computing and the Grid, 2009. CCGRID'09. 9th IEEE/ACM International Symposium on* (pp. 124-131). IEEE. 10.1109/CCGRID.2009.93

Rocha, F., Abreu, S., & Correia, M. (2013a). *The Next Frontier: Managing Data Confidentiality and Integrity in the Cloud*. IEEE Computer Society Press.

Sailer, R., Zhang, X., Jaeger, T., & Van Doorn, L. (2004, August). Design and Implementation of a TCG-based Integrity Measurement Architecture. In USENIX Security symposium (Vol. 13, pp. 223-238). USENIX.

Singh, S., Jeong, Y. S., & Park, J. H. (2016). A survey on cloud computing security: Issues, threats, and solutions. *Journal of Network and Computer Applications*, *75*, 200–222. doi:10.1016/j.jnca.2016.09.002

Stallings, W. (2010a). Cryptography and Network Security: Principles and Practice. Prentice Hall Press.

Chapter 6
Results and Discussions

ABSTRACT

This chapter describes the proof-of-concept of the proposed protocol architecture. The eXtensible modular hypervisor framework has been utilized to build the TrustVisor hypervisor along with the core modules: cryptography operations, TEE, and TPM emulator, which contains TPM library function to make a secure communication with TPM hardware. The constructed hypervisor has been placed in the cloud server grub entry to make a choice of hypervisor. To ensure the trust worthiness of cloud platform, a remote attestation concept is used along with the most popular and widely used method called integrity measurement architecture (IMA). Remote attestation uses IMA. It works based on binary attestation concept. After configuring IMA, it calculates and extends the hashes of all components while boot process into their respective PCRs. To ensure the remote attestation with privacy preserving of NC, the authors used attestation identity key (AIK) for signing hashes of PCRs while performing quote operation. They used TPM emulator for communication with TPM device using TPM driver.

PERFORMANCE OF TPM COMMANDS

As discussed earlier, we used open source cloud software called eucalyptus to establish an IaaS private cloud for our testing. Eucalyptus consists well defined components such as node controller, cloud controller, walrus, storage controller and cluster controller, those provides efficient communication among resources using web-service. Eucalyptus is an EC2 API-compatible and which is an answer to commercial Amazon EC2 cloud infrastructure. Eucalyptus supports libvirt hypervisor, it consists most popular hypervisors Xen and KVM hypervisors. The

DOI: 10.4018/978-1-5225-7924-3.ch006

eucalyptus components are well defined with web-service based interfaces and those components are developed using high-level and standard packages such as Axis2, Apache, and Rampart . Our proposed architecture utilizes these components to prove that our concept is secure from insider attacks.

The node controller is the central component of our proposed eucalyptus cloud frame work, where cloud controller can launch and execute virtual machines. The proposed framework implemented on HP elite Notebook 8540 with configuration of Intel i5 processor, 8GB RAM, 500HDD and Ubuntu 12.04 as a host OS. The Eucalyptus cloud software used for implementing the private cloud that provides an infrastructure for launching virtual machine's. The experimental results show that proposed framework has greater ability to reduce the TCB minimization and less over heads while communicate with TPM device through the host operating system.The Intel SENTER (AMD SKINIT) instruction takes 20.5ms for the initiation of secure boot along with the TrustVisor hypervisor boot process. The PCR Extend is used to quote respective PCR value and it took 10.68ms. The TPM quote for measuring the PCR values with hash values are calculated and replaced with new hash digest and this operation took 357.68ms. Thus, it shows us that Flicker based environment takes long time to respond for the TPM quote. The seal and unseal operation takes 45.29ms and 537.87ms, when compared to other hypervisor performance in both operations TrustVisor has great ability to reduce the overheads in unseal operation.

The remote attestation took 100.3ms for trusting the platform using the PCR values with cryptographic techniques those we discussed earlier sections. The results show us that TrustVisor has great ability to reduce the overheads during the TPM operations.

The Table 1 illustrates the performance of TrustVisor on cloud environment. HMAC is used to generate the hash digest of software status in PCR registers.

Figure 1. TPM performance evaluation (ms)

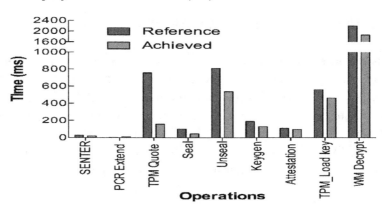

Table 1. HMAC and basic operations on TrustVisor (ms)

	Extend	Seal	Unseal	Quote
Native Linux	24066	358102	1008654	815654
TrustVisor	533	11.7	12.6	21000
	HMAC		Sign	
	Avg	Stdev	Avg	Stdev
Flicker	62.644	0.181	67.461	0.008
TrustVisor	0.051	0.003	5.012	0.018

Those registers are used for integrity check of client virtual machines contents. The avg and standard deviation is calculated on TrustVisor and Flicker. Flicker takes 62.644ms where as TrustVisor takes 0.059ms, it indicates the performance and dependent nature of execution of cloud components on node controller. In this way, we can calculate the start deviation of both components are: 0.003ms and 0.181ms respectively. It leverages the potentiality of TrustVisor in cloud environment. Such that this can work with high performance in execution point of view as well as in implementation of cloud components. The TrustVisor design disabled with MMU-based mechanism along with nested page table concept in the AMD specific x86 untrusted legacy operating systems. The nested page table maintains separate page for both host system (hPT) as well as guest operating system (gPT). Hence, the TrustVisor provides an isolated execution environment along with PAL.

SECURE VM LAUNCH

In this section, we describe secure VM launch approach in cloud infrastructure using TPM remote attestation on TrustVisor and the previous chapter describes about how application are executed in isolated environment on top of the TrustVisor.

Table 2. LOC comparison with other hypervisors

Hypervisor	Hypapp	XMHF Core	Total
TrustVisor	3939	6018	9957
LockDown	9391	6018	15409
XTRec	3500	6018	9518
SecVisor	2200	6018	8218

Figure 2. TCB comparison

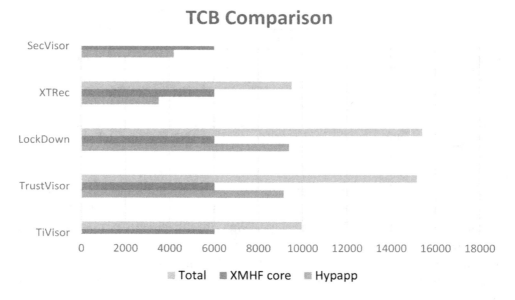

This mechanism achieves the data integrity of client applications which are running on trusted hypervisor. An external trusted third party or verifier receives a TPM-generated attestation that includes set of PCR values and following data that have to be extended to convey the following information:

- SKINIT instruction (AMD) used in bootstrap for the execution of TrustVisor using dynamic root trust.
- Next, TrustVisor receives the control of dynamic root of trust.
- One of the PCRs contains cryptographic hash (measurement) of TrustVisor
- TrustVisor generates the identity key using current TPM AIK for µTPM.

A TrustVisor attestation consists set of outputs of HV_quote operation along with other untrusted data to the verifier making sense out of the µPCRs. The trusted party or verifier must trust the TrustVisor using TPM attestation service. Suppose TrustVisor is untrusted, then entire cloud environment can be considering as untrusted. Such that, no trust environment can be constructed with untrusted TrustVisor.

The client VM stored in encrypted form in Cloud Storage such that VM can be executed on NCs, those equipped with TPM device and drivers. The secure VM ensures that decryption key from client is securely taken by using proposed protocol. The proposed secure VM launch protocol, obtains decryption key from the client and decrypt the VM on NC in presence of user. The secure launch is proceeds in two stages: in the first stage we verify the public key of TrustVior (pk_t) and client (pk$_c$). This can be achieved by using client TPM and NC to provide secure channel among client and TrustVisor using Flicker secure channel protocol. The first stage as proceeds: the client sends a VM request to the NC for creation of VM or VM launch. Upon receiving the request from client, NC initiates the TrustVisor and executes the Piece of Application Logic (PAL). The PCR 18 extends with measurement of PAL and its respective input and output. Here, PAL is a tiny application that isolates the execution environment, supports the VM decryption and generates the asymmetric key for TrustVisor.

In this section, we explained proposed architecture proof -of-concept with implementation. As we discussed earlier, remote attestation used for verification of VM by external trusted parties. This approach mainly used Intel based processor called Integrity Measurement Architecture (IMA). Our proof of concept proposed algorithm uses TPM secure VM launch protocol for securing the VM in Cloud Storage (CS). The VM kernels are encrypted and stored in cloud storage, so that only trusted or verified NCs can launch the VM. The process of secure VM launch ensures that client private key or decryption key is provided to NC to decrypt the VM. The proposed protocol proceeds as follows: the client sent VM request to NC and initialize TrustVisor session and extends the PCR register 18 with measurement of TrustVisor. TrustVisor consists of private and public key for session management and secure VM launch operation. TrustVisor sends public key (tpk) to node controller and node controller forward a key along with nonce of client. Client responds with nonce, client private key and public key of Trust visor to the Node controller and the Node Controller forwards the same copy of keys to the Trust visor.

Upon receiving, the TrustVisor decrypt the VM kernel image using private key of client and public key of TrustVisor. Now, a VM execution started in isolated environment apart from the Node controller.

REMOTE ATTESTATION

As described in earlier sections, TPM module stores the measurement in PCR registers and those are utilized for remote verification by extending PCR registers. An actual process starts by invoking nonce to Node controller and the node controller forwards respective PCR value to the third party for verification. The third party matches the PCR hash value with earlier PCR value. Upon matching NC request the client for private key and client send the private key back to node controller for the decryption of VM. After receiving key from client, node controller decrypts the VM kernel and establishes a session in TrustVisorfor isolated environment.

Figure 3 and 4 shows the secure VM launch and remote attestation protocol respectively. The main issue with the earlier mechanism (Park at al., 2015) is that client can occasionally or periodically freezing for approximately for very 550ms in the remote attestation phase. This issue hurts the cloud consumer while performing the remote attestation with cloud server.

The issue is because of poor TPM operations such as TPM_Quote2. Such that, we replace heavy operations with minimal operations in the software cryptographic operations for attestation protocol. To analyze the performance of remote attestation, TrustVisor uses a 1024-bit session key, which is created or generated in boot process. The below table shows, the performance of various hypervisors. The Native Linux takes 518.1ms, TGVisor takes 172.1ms, TrustVisor takes 288.3ms, SecVisor takes 240.5ms, Lockdown takes 298.3ms and Proposed framework with TrustVisor takes 169.8ms. Hence, the TrustVisor takes less time for remote attestation for the remote attestation.

As shown in the Figure 5, the proposed framework protocol in the remote attestation outperforms the earlier hypervisors by 2.88 times because the proposed framework uses light TPM operations such as TPM_PCR_Extend and TPM_PCR_Extend to check or verify the integrity of the infrastructure where virtual machines to be executed or being executing. The TPM_PCR_Read takes 7.2ms and TPM_PCR_Extend takes 8.2ms to update the PCR register. Such the TPM operations takes less amount overheads while performing the remote attestation with remote party.

Figure 3. Secure VM launch

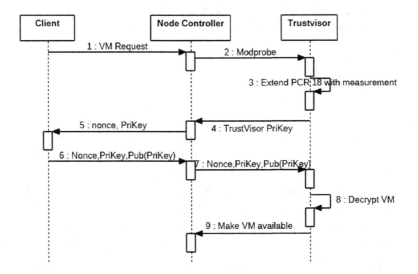

Figure 4. Remote Attestation

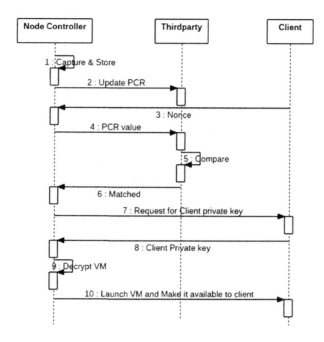

Figure 5. Remote attestation evolution(ms)

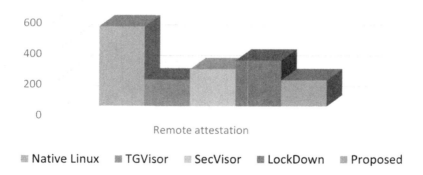

Table 3. Performance evolution of remote attestation (ms)

Native Linux	TGVisor	CloudVisor	SecVisor	Lockdown	Proposed
518.1	172.1	288.3	240.5	298.3	169.8

SUMMARY

In this chapter the results are evaluated with earlier virtualization layer designs. The proposed framework takes less amount of CPU time to execute the commands those are performed when trusted computing techniques are under execution. The Trusted computing base of the proposed framework is reduced by eliminating expensive cryptographic operations. The remote attestation takes less amount of time to prove the trustworthiness of cloud resources. The experimental results clearly show that proposed framework can prevent insider attacks using PAL and it can detect the abnormalities of the insiders by using Integrity Measurement Architecture. Such that the proposed framework can effectively prevent and detect the insider attacks in the cloud infrastructure.

Conclusion

The due to the cloud computing characteristics and flexibilities, everyone is moving towards the utilization of cloud computing services. But, the biggest challenge is to secure the consumer private or sensitive data. The main aim of this research is to protect sensitive data from internal breaches i.e., from insiders or employee of cloud service provider. The proposed framework provides an integrity and confidentiality with trusted hypervisor using trusted cloud computing techniques. The proposed framework includes secure virtual machines launch protocol which allows the cloud consumer to verify the data as well as platform integrity and it performs the confidentiality checking of computation data in the cloud environment using piece of application logic. The trusted computing base of the proposed protocol is less than earlier methods, in which we excluded most of the cryptographic operations to reduce the trusted computing base. The evaluation results show that the proposed framework is practical and reducing the execution of critical commands in the cloud environment.

FUTURE SCOPE

The trustworthy architecture we have suggested further reductions of hypervisor trusted computing base. The fact is that Xen is a monolithic virtual machines monitor means it has a considerably high number of lines of code when compared with micro-hypervisor approaches such as the NOVA hypervisor. Further reducing the trusted computing base of the trustworthy cloud computing architecture would mean disaggregating Xen or using a micro hypervisor to take advantage of the protection rings in root-mode. These protection rings could be used to isolate virtual machines monitors launched for each individual virtual machine. This means that the critical parts of the hypervisor would execute in root-mode's ring 0 while the less privilege operations could execute in root-mode's ring 3. A virtual machine's guest operating system and its applications would use non-root mode's ring 0 and ring 3, respectively. In such an architecture, the privilege operations currently isolated in a special-purpose virtual machines could be moved to root-mode's ring 3. This change means a mandatory memory access control mechanism can be implemented in a more appropriate way starting from the design stage of a secure micro-hypervisor architecture.

Related Readings

To continue IGI Global's long-standing tradition of advancing innovation through emerging research, please find below a compiled list of recommended IGI Global book chapters and journal articles in the areas of cloud architecture, cloud computing, and internet security. These related readings will provide additional information and guidance to further enrich your knowledge and assist you with your own research.

A., U. B. (2018). High Efficient Data Embedding in Image Steganography Using Parallel Programming. In P. Karthikeyan, & M. Thangavel (Eds.), *Applications of Security, Mobile, Analytic, and Cloud (SMAC) Technologies for Effective Information Processing and Management* (pp. 67-80). Hershey, PA: IGI Global. doi:10.4018/978-1-5225-4044-1.ch004

Abdelhamid, M., Venkatesan, S., Gaia, J., & Sharman, R. (2018). Do Privacy Concerns Affect Information Seeking via Smartphones? In M. Gupta, R. Sharman, J. Walp, & P. Mulgund (Eds.), *Information Technology Risk Management and Compliance in Modern Organizations* (pp. 301–314). Hershey, PA: IGI Global. doi:10.4018/978-1-5225-2604-9.ch011

Abirami, A. M., Askarunisa, A., Shiva Shankari, R. A., & Revathy, R. (2018). Ontology Based Feature Extraction From Text Documents. In P. Karthikeyan & M. Thangavel (Eds.), *Applications of Security, Mobile, Analytic, and Cloud (SMAC) Technologies for Effective Information Processing and Management* (pp. 174–195). Hershey, PA: IGI Global. doi:10.4018/978-1-5225-4044-1.ch009

Adeel, M. (2016). Big Data Virtualization and Visualization: On the Cloud. In R. Kannan, R. Rasool, H. Jin, & S. Balasundaram (Eds.), *Managing and Processing Big Data in Cloud Computing* (pp. 168–184). Hershey, PA: IGI Global. doi:10.4018/978-1-4666-9767-6.ch012

Adhikari, M., Das, A., & Mukherjee, A. (2016). Utility Computing and Its Utilization. In G. Deka, G. Siddesh, K. Srinivasa, & L. Patnaik (Eds.), *Emerging Research Surrounding Power Consumption and Performance Issues in Utility Computing* (pp. 1–21). Hershey, PA: IGI Global. doi:10.4018/978-1-4666-8853-7.ch001

Adhikari, M., & Kar, S. (2016). Advanced Topics GPU Programming and CUDA Architecture. In G. Deka, G. Siddesh, K. Srinivasa, & L. Patnaik (Eds.), *Emerging Research Surrounding Power Consumption and Performance Issues in Utility Computing* (pp. 175–203). Hershey, PA: IGI Global. doi:10.4018/978-1-4666-8853-7.ch008

Adhikari, M., & Roy, D. (2016). Green Computing. In G. Deka, G. Siddesh, K. Srinivasa, & L. Patnaik (Eds.), *Emerging Research Surrounding Power Consumption and Performance Issues in Utility Computing* (pp. 84–108). Hershey, PA: IGI Global. doi:10.4018/978-1-4666-8853-7.ch005

Ahmad, F. (2016). Big Data Virtualization and Visualization on Cloud. In R. Kannan, R. Rasool, H. Jin, & S. Balasundaram (Eds.), *Managing and Processing Big Data in Cloud Computing* (pp. 145–155). Hershey, PA: IGI Global. doi:10.4018/978-1-4666-9767-6.ch010

Ahmad, K., Kumar, G., Wahid, A., & Kirmani, M. M. (2016). Software Performance Estimate using Fuzzy Based Backpropagation Learning. In G. Deka, G. Siddesh, K. Srinivasa, & L. Patnaik (Eds.), *Emerging Research Surrounding Power Consumption and Performance Issues in Utility Computing* (pp. 320–344). Hershey, PA: IGI Global. doi:10.4018/978-1-4666-8853-7.ch016

Alling, A., Powers, N. R., & Soyata, T. (2016). Face Recognition: A Tutorial on Computational Aspects. In G. Deka, G. Siddesh, K. Srinivasa, & L. Patnaik (Eds.), *Emerging Research Surrounding Power Consumption and Performance Issues in Utility Computing* (pp. 405–425). Hershey, PA: IGI Global. doi:10.4018/978-1-4666-8853-7.ch020

Alohali, B. (2017). Detection Protocol of Possible Crime Scenes Using Internet of Things (IoT). In M. Moore (Ed.), *Cybersecurity Breaches and Issues Surrounding Online Threat Protection* (pp. 175–196). Hershey, PA: IGI Global. doi:10.4018/978-1-5225-1941-6.ch008

Alotaibi, R., Ramachandran, M., Kor, A., & Hosseinian-Far, A. (2016). Adoption of Social Media as Communication Channels in Government Agencies. In Z. Mahmood (Ed.), *Cloud Computing Technologies for Connected Government* (pp. 39–73). Hershey, PA: IGI Global. doi:10.4018/978-1-4666-8629-8.ch003

Ammari, H. M., Shaout, A., & Mustapha, F. (2017). Sensing Coverage in Three-Dimensional Space: A Survey. In N. Ray & A. Turuk (Eds.), *Handbook of Research on Advanced Wireless Sensor Network Applications, Protocols, and Architectures* (pp. 1–28). Hershey, PA: IGI Global. doi:10.4018/978-1-5225-0486-3.ch001

Anshari, M., & Almunawar, M. N. (2016). E-Government Initiatives through Cloud Computing: Empowering Citizens. In Z. Mahmood (Ed.), *Cloud Computing Technologies for Connected Government* (pp. 74–92). Hershey, PA: IGI Global. doi:10.4018/978-1-4666-8629-8.ch004

Anwar, H., Shibli, M. A., & Habiba, U. (2016). An Extensible Identity Management Framework for Cloud-Based E-Government Systems. In Z. Mahmood (Ed.), *Cloud Computing Technologies for Connected Government* (pp. 163–187). Hershey, PA: IGI Global. doi:10.4018/978-1-4666-8629-8.ch007

Armstrong, S., & Yampolskiy, R. V. (2017). Security Solutions for Intelligent and Complex Systems. In M. Dawson, M. Eltayeb, & M. Omar (Eds.), *Security Solutions for Hyperconnectivity and the Internet of Things* (pp. 37–88). Hershey, PA: IGI Global. doi:10.4018/978-1-5225-0741-3.ch003

Ashraf, U., Rizvi, S. S., & Azeem, M. F. (2016). Performance Evaluation of Routing Metrics in Wireless Multi-Hop Networks. In R. Kannan, R. Rasool, H. Jin, & S. Balasundaram (Eds.), *Managing and Processing Big Data in Cloud Computing* (pp. 85–104). Hershey, PA: IGI Global. doi:10.4018/978-1-4666-9767-6.ch006

Atli, D. (2017). Cybercrimes via Virtual Currencies in International Business. In M. Moore (Ed.), *Cybersecurity Breaches and Issues Surrounding Online Threat Protection* (pp. 121–143). Hershey, PA: IGI Global. doi:10.4018/978-1-5225-1941-6.ch006

Bamrara, A. (2017). Identifying and Analyzing the Latent Cyber Threats in Developing Economies. In M. Moore (Ed.), *Cybersecurity Breaches and Issues Surrounding Online Threat Protection* (pp. 74–94). Hershey, PA: IGI Global. doi:10.4018/978-1-5225-1941-6.ch004

Bandopadhaya, S., & Roy, J. S. (2017). Spectral Efficiency in Wireless Networks through MIMO-OFDM System. In N. Ray & A. Turuk (Eds.), *Handbook of Research on Advanced Wireless Sensor Network Applications, Protocols, and Architectures* (pp. 249–277). Hershey, PA: IGI Global. doi:10.4018/978-1-5225-0486-3.ch010

Benadda, M., Bouamrane, K., & Belalem, G. (2017). How to Manage Persons Taken Malaise at the Steering Wheel Using HAaaS in a Vehicular Cloud Computing Environment. *International Journal of Ambient Computing and Intelligence*, 8(2), 70–87. doi:10.4018/IJACI.2017040105

Bhadoria, R. S. (2016). Performance of Enterprise Architecture in Utility Computing. In G. Deka, G. Siddesh, K. Srinivasa, & L. Patnaik (Eds.), *Emerging Research Surrounding Power Consumption and Performance Issues in Utility Computing* (pp. 44–68). Hershey, PA: IGI Global. doi:10.4018/978-1-4666-8853-7.ch003

Bhadoria, R. S., & Patil, C. (2016). Adaptive Mobile Architecture with Utility Computing. In G. Deka, G. Siddesh, K. Srinivasa, & L. Patnaik (Eds.), *Emerging Research Surrounding Power Consumption and Performance Issues in Utility Computing* (pp. 386–404). Hershey, PA: IGI Global. doi:10.4018/978-1-4666-8853-7.ch019

Bhardwaj, A. (2017). Solutions for Securing End User Data over the Cloud Deployed Applications. In M. Moore (Ed.), *Cybersecurity Breaches and Issues Surrounding Online Threat Protection* (pp. 198–218). Hershey, PA: IGI Global. doi:10.4018/978-1-5225-1941-6.ch009

Bhargavi, K., & Babu, B. S. (2016). GPU Computation and Platforms. In G. Deka, G. Siddesh, K. Srinivasa, & L. Patnaik (Eds.), *Emerging Research Surrounding Power Consumption and Performance Issues in Utility Computing* (pp. 136–174). Hershey, PA: IGI Global. doi:10.4018/978-1-4666-8853-7.ch007

Bhattacharjee, J., Sengupta, A., Barik, M. S., & Mazumdar, C. (2018). An Analytical Study of Methodologies and Tools for Enterprise Information Security Risk Management. In M. Gupta, R. Sharman, J. Walp, & P. Mulgund (Eds.), *Information Technology Risk Management and Compliance in Modern Organizations* (pp. 1–20). Hershey, PA: IGI Global. doi:10.4018/978-1-5225-2604-9.ch001

Cano, J., & Hernández, R. (2017). Managing Software Architecture in Domains of Security-Critical Systems: Multifaceted Collaborative eGovernment Projects. In S. Zoughbi (Ed.), *Securing Government Information and Data in Developing Countries* (pp. 1–26). Hershey, PA: IGI Global. doi:10.4018/978-1-5225-1703-0.ch001

Cardenas-Haro, J. A., & Dawson, M. (2017). Tails Linux Operating System: The Amnesiac Incognito System in Times of High Surveillance, Its Security Flaws, Limitations, and Strengths in the Fight for Democracy. In M. Dawson, M. Eltayeb, & M. Omar (Eds.), *Security Solutions for Hyperconnectivity and the Internet of Things* (pp. 260–271). Hershey, PA: IGI Global. doi:10.4018/978-1-5225-0741-3.ch010

Cardoso, A., Moreira, F., & Simões, P. (2016). A Support Framework for the Migration of E-Government Services to the Cloud. In Z. Mahmood (Ed.), *Cloud Computing Technologies for Connected Government* (pp. 124–162). Hershey, PA: IGI Global. doi:10.4018/978-1-4666-8629-8.ch006

Chaudhari, G., & Mulgund, P. (2018). Strengthening IT Governance With COBIT 5. In M. Gupta, R. Sharman, J. Walp, & P. Mulgund (Eds.), *Information Technology Risk Management and Compliance in Modern Organizations* (pp. 48–69). Hershey, PA: IGI Global. doi:10.4018/978-1-5225-2604-9.ch003

Chen, C. K., & Almunawar, M. N. (2016). Cost Benefits of Cloud Computing for Connected Government. In Z. Mahmood (Ed.), *Cloud Computing Technologies for Connected Government* (pp. 345–368). Hershey, PA: IGI Global. doi:10.4018/978-1-4666-8629-8.ch014

Dahal, S., & Ray, N. K. (2017). Intrusion Detection in MANET for Network Layer. In N. Ray & A. Turuk (Eds.), *Handbook of Research on Advanced Wireless Sensor Network Applications, Protocols, and Architectures* (pp. 326–352). Hershey, PA: IGI Global. doi:10.4018/978-1-5225-0486-3.ch013

Dale, M. (2016). Putting Implementation into Enterprise Architecture Research. *International Journal of Enterprise Information Systems*, *12*(2), 14–25. doi:10.4018/IJEIS.2016040102

Das, P. K. (2016). Comparative Study on XEN, KVM, VSphere, and Hyper-V. In G. Deka, G. Siddesh, K. Srinivasa, & L. Patnaik (Eds.), *Emerging Research Surrounding Power Consumption and Performance Issues in Utility Computing* (pp. 233–261). Hershey, PA: IGI Global. doi:10.4018/978-1-4666-8853-7.ch011

Das, P. K., & Deka, G. C. (2016). History and Evolution of GPU Architecture. In G. Deka, G. Siddesh, K. Srinivasa, & L. Patnaik (Eds.), *Emerging Research Surrounding Power Consumption and Performance Issues in Utility Computing* (pp. 109–135). Hershey, PA: IGI Global. doi:10.4018/978-1-4666-8853-7.ch006

Dass, S., & Prabhu, J. (2018). Amelioration of Big Data Analytics by Employing Big Data Tools and Techniques. In P. Karthikeyan & M. Thangavel (Eds.), *Applications of Security, Mobile, Analytic, and Cloud (SMAC) Technologies for Effective Information Processing and Management* (pp. 212–232). Hershey, PA: IGI Global. doi:10.4018/978-1-5225-4044-1.ch011

Dawson, M. (2017). Exploring Secure Computing for the Internet of Things, Internet of Everything, Web of Things, and Hyperconnectivity. In M. Dawson, M. Eltayeb, & M. Omar (Eds.), *Security Solutions for Hyperconnectivity and the Internet of Things* (pp. 1–12). Hershey, PA: IGI Global. doi:10.4018/978-1-5225-0741-3.ch001

Easton, J., & Parmar, R. (2017). Navigating Your Way to the Hybrid Cloud. In J. Chen, Y. Zhang, & R. Gottschalk (Eds.), *Handbook of Research on End-to-End Cloud Computing Architecture Design* (pp. 15–38). Hershey, PA: IGI Global. doi:10.4018/978-1-5225-0759-8.ch002

Egwutuoha, I. P., & Chen, S. (2017). Cost of Using Cloud Computing: HaaS vs. IaaS. In J. Chen, Y. Zhang, & R. Gottschalk (Eds.), *Handbook of Research on End-to-End Cloud Computing Architecture Design* (pp. 455–472). Hershey, PA: IGI Global. doi:10.4018/978-1-5225-0759-8.ch018

Ehrhardt, R. (2017). Cloud Build Methodology. In J. Chen, Y. Zhang, & R. Gottschalk (Eds.), *Handbook of Research on End-to-End Cloud Computing Architecture Design* (pp. 105–129). Hershey, PA: IGI Global. doi:10.4018/978-1-5225-0759-8.ch006

Eigenbrode, S., & Nassar, S. (2017). Design and Implementation of Service Management in DevOps Enabled Cloud Computing Models. In J. Chen, Y. Zhang, & R. Gottschalk (Eds.), *Handbook of Research on End-to-End Cloud Computing Architecture Design* (pp. 326–347). Hershey, PA: IGI Global. doi:10.4018/978-1-5225-0759-8.ch014

El Alami, H., & Najid, A. (2017). (SET) Smart Energy Management and Throughput Maximization: A New Routing Protocol for WSNs. In K. Munir (Ed.), *Security Management in Mobile Cloud Computing* (pp. 1–28). Hershey, PA: IGI Global. doi:10.4018/978-1-5225-0602-7.ch001

El Moussaid, N., & Toumanari, A. (2017). A Cloud Intrusion Detection Based on Classification of Activities and Mobile Agent. In K. Munir (Ed.), *Security Management in Mobile Cloud Computing* (pp. 29–42). Hershey, PA: IGI Global. doi:10.4018/978-1-5225-0602-7.ch002

Elkabbany, G. F., & Rasslan, M. (2017). Security Issues in Distributed Computing System Models. In M. Dawson, M. Eltayeb, & M. Omar (Eds.), *Security Solutions for Hyperconnectivity and the Internet of Things* (pp. 211–259). Hershey, PA: IGI Global. doi:10.4018/978-1-5225-0741-3.ch009

Elkhodr, M., Shahrestani, S., & Cheung, H. (2017). Internet of Things Research Challenges. In M. Dawson, M. Eltayeb, & M. Omar (Eds.), *Security Solutions for Hyperconnectivity and the Internet of Things* (pp. 13–36). Hershey, PA: IGI Global. doi:10.4018/978-1-5225-0741-3.ch002

Eltayeb, M. (2017). Privacy and Security. In M. Dawson, M. Eltayeb, & M. Omar (Eds.), *Security Solutions for Hyperconnectivity and the Internet of Things* (pp. 89–112). Hershey, PA: IGI Global. doi:10.4018/978-1-5225-0741-3.ch004

Erdenebold, T. (2017). A Smart Government Framework for Mobile Application Services in Mongolia. In S. Zoughbi (Ed.), *Securing Government Information and Data in Developing Countries* (pp. 90–103). Hershey, PA: IGI Global. doi:10.4018/978-1-5225-1703-0.ch005

Related Readings

Erturk, E. (2017). Cloud Computing and Cybersecurity Issues Facing Local Enterprises. In M. Moore (Ed.), *Cybersecurity Breaches and Issues Surrounding Online Threat Protection* (pp. 219–247). Hershey, PA: IGI Global. doi:10.4018/978-1-5225-1941-6.ch010

Fatima, K., & Majeed, H. (2016). Texture-Based Evolutionary Method for Cancer Classification in Histopathology. In R. Kannan, R. Rasool, H. Jin, & S. Balasundaram (Eds.), *Managing and Processing Big Data in Cloud Computing* (pp. 55–69). Hershey, PA: IGI Global. doi:10.4018/978-1-4666-9767-6.ch004

Gahlawat, M., & Sharma, P. (2016). Green, Energy-Efficient Computing and Sustainability Issues in Cloud. In R. Kannan, R. Rasool, H. Jin, & S. Balasundaram (Eds.), *Managing and Processing Big Data in Cloud Computing* (pp. 206–217). Hershey, PA: IGI Global. doi:10.4018/978-1-4666-9767-6.ch014

Ghany, K. K., & Zawbaa, H. M. (2017). Hybrid Biometrics and Watermarking Authentication. In S. Zoughbi (Ed.), *Securing Government Information and Data in Developing Countries* (pp. 37–61). Hershey, PA: IGI Global. doi:10.4018/978-1-5225-1703-0.ch003

Goher, S. Z., Javed, B., & Bloodsworth, P. (2016). A Survey of Cloud-Based Services Leveraged by Big Data Applications. In R. Kannan, R. Rasool, H. Jin, & S. Balasundaram (Eds.), *Managing and Processing Big Data in Cloud Computing* (pp. 121–131). Hershey, PA: IGI Global. doi:10.4018/978-1-4666-9767-6.ch008

Hallappanavar, V. L., & Birje, M. N. (2017). Trust Management in Cloud Computing. In M. Dawson, M. Eltayeb, & M. Omar (Eds.), *Security Solutions for Hyperconnectivity and the Internet of Things* (pp. 151–183). Hershey, PA: IGI Global. doi:10.4018/978-1-5225-0741-3.ch007

Hamidine, H., & Mahmood, A. (2017). Cloud Computing Data Storage Security Based on Different Encryption Schemes. In J. Chen, Y. Zhang, & R. Gottschalk (Eds.), *Handbook of Research on End-to-End Cloud Computing Architecture Design* (pp. 189–221). Hershey, PA: IGI Global. doi:10.4018/978-1-5225-0759-8.ch009

Hemalatha, J., KavithaDevi, M.K., & Geetha, S. (2018). A Recent Study on High Dimensional Features Used in Stego Image Anomaly Detection. In P. Karthikeyan & M. Thangavel (Eds.), Applications of Security, Mobile, Analytic, and Cloud (SMAC) Technologies for Effective Information Processing and Management (pp. 49-66). Hershey, PA: IGI Global. doi:10.4018/978-1-5225-4044-1.ch003

Hinton, H. (2017). Security and Compliance: IaaS, PaaS, and Hybrid Cloud. In J. Chen, Y. Zhang, & R. Gottschalk (Eds.), *Handbook of Research on End-to-End Cloud Computing Architecture Design* (pp. 159–188). Hershey, PA: IGI Global. doi:10.4018/978-1-5225-0759-8.ch008

Hu, W., Kaabouch, N., Guo, H., & ElSaid, A. A. (2018). Location-Based Advertising Using Location-Aware Data Mining. In P. Karthikeyan & M. Thangavel (Eds.), *Applications of Security, Mobile, Analytic, and Cloud (SMAC) Technologies for Effective Information Processing and Management* (pp. 196–211). Hershey, PA: IGI Global. doi:10.4018/978-1-5225-4044-1.ch010

Husain, M. S., & Khan, N. (2017). Big Data on E-Government. In S. Zoughbi (Ed.), *Securing Government Information and Data in Developing Countries* (pp. 27–36). Hershey, PA: IGI Global. doi:10.4018/978-1-5225-1703-0.ch002

Husain, M. S., & Khanum, M. A. (2017). Cloud Computing in E-Governance: Indian Perspective. In S. Zoughbi (Ed.), *Securing Government Information and Data in Developing Countries* (pp. 104–114). Hershey, PA: IGI Global. doi:10.4018/978-1-5225-1703-0.ch006

Jadon, K. S., Mudgal, P., & Bhadoria, R. S. (2016). Optimization and Management of Resource in Utility Computing. In G. Deka, G. Siddesh, K. Srinivasa, & L. Patnaik (Eds.), *Emerging Research Surrounding Power Consumption and Performance Issues in Utility Computing* (pp. 22–43). Hershey, PA: IGI Global. doi:10.4018/978-1-4666-8853-7.ch002

Jain, P., & Pang, Y. (2017). Cloud Computing Architectural Patterns. In J. Chen, Y. Zhang, & R. Gottschalk (Eds.), *Handbook of Research on End-to-End Cloud Computing Architecture Design* (pp. 56–72). Hershey, PA: IGI Global. doi:10.4018/978-1-5225-0759-8.ch004

Jaluka, R. (2017). Enterprise IT Transformation Using Cloud Service Broker. In J. Chen, Y. Zhang, & R. Gottschalk (Eds.), *Handbook of Research on End-to-End Cloud Computing Architecture Design* (pp. 348–375). Hershey, PA: IGI Global. doi:10.4018/978-1-5225-0759-8.ch015

Jena, G. C. (2017). Multi-Sensor Data Fusion (MSDF). In N. Ray & A. Turuk (Eds.), *Handbook of Research on Advanced Wireless Sensor Network Applications, Protocols, and Architectures* (pp. 29–61). Hershey, PA: IGI Global. doi:10.4018/978-1-5225-0486-3.ch002

Kasemsap, K. (2017). Robotics: Theory and Applications. In M. Moore (Ed.), *Cybersecurity Breaches and Issues Surrounding Online Threat Protection* (pp. 311–345). Hershey, PA: IGI Global. doi:10.4018/978-1-5225-1941-6.ch013

Khadtare, M. S. (2016). GPU Based Image Quality Assessment using Structural Similarity (SSIM) Index. In G. Deka, G. Siddesh, K. Srinivasa, & L. Patnaik (Eds.), *Emerging Research Surrounding Power Consumption and Performance Issues in Utility Computing* (pp. 276–282). Hershey, PA: IGI Global. doi:10.4018/978-1-4666-8853-7.ch013

Khandelwal, P., & Somani, G. (2017). Virtual Machine Placement in IaaS Cloud. In J. Chen, Y. Zhang, & R. Gottschalk (Eds.), *Handbook of Research on End-to-End Cloud Computing Architecture Design* (pp. 130–158). Hershey, PA: IGI Global. doi:10.4018/978-1-5225-0759-8.ch007

Kiran, M. (2016). Legal Issues Surrounding Connected Government Services: A Closer Look at G-Clouds. In Z. Mahmood (Ed.), *Cloud Computing Technologies for Connected Government* (pp. 322–344). Hershey, PA: IGI Global. doi:10.4018/978-1-4666-8629-8.ch013

Krishnamachariar, P. K., & Gupta, M. (2018). Swimming Upstream in Turbulent Waters: Auditing Agile Development. In M. Gupta, R. Sharman, J. Walp, & P. Mulgund (Eds.), *Information Technology Risk Management and Compliance in Modern Organizations* (pp. 268–300). Hershey, PA: IGI Global. doi:10.4018/978-1-5225-2604-9.ch010

Kuada, E. (2017). Security and Trust in Cloud Computing. In M. Dawson, M. Eltayeb, & M. Omar (Eds.), *Security Solutions for Hyperconnectivity and the Internet of Things* (pp. 184–210). Hershey, PA: IGI Global. doi:10.4018/978-1-5225-0741-3.ch008

Kumar, M. S., & Prabhu, J. (2018). Recent Development in Big Data Analytics: Research Perspective. In P. Karthikeyan & M. Thangavel (Eds.), *Applications of Security, Mobile, Analytic, and Cloud (SMAC) Technologies for Effective Information Processing and Management* (pp. 233–257). Hershey, PA: IGI Global. doi:10.4018/978-1-5225-4044-1.ch012

Kumar, N., & Singh, Y. (2017). Routing Protocols in Wireless Sensor Networks. In N. Ray & A. Turuk (Eds.), *Handbook of Research on Advanced Wireless Sensor Network Applications, Protocols, and Architectures* (pp. 86–128). Hershey, PA: IGI Global. doi:10.4018/978-1-5225-0486-3.ch004

Kumar, V., & Kumar, R. (2017). Prevention of Blackhole Attack using Certificateless Signature (CLS) Scheme in MANET. In M. Dawson, M. Eltayeb, & M. Omar (Eds.), *Security Solutions for Hyperconnectivity and the Internet of Things* (pp. 130–150). Hershey, PA: IGI Global. doi:10.4018/978-1-5225-0741-3.ch006

Lahmiri, S. (2018). Information Technology Outsourcing Risk Factors and Provider Selection. In M. Gupta, R. Sharman, J. Walp, & P. Mulgund (Eds.), *Information Technology Risk Management and Compliance in Modern Organizations* (pp. 214–228). Hershey, PA: IGI Global. doi:10.4018/978-1-5225-2604-9.ch008

Lee, J., Eapen, A. M., Akbar, M. S., & Rao, H. R. (2017). An Exploration Regarding Issues in Insider Threat. In M. Moore (Ed.), *Cybersecurity Breaches and Issues Surrounding Online Threat Protection* (pp. 1–23). Hershey, PA: IGI Global. doi:10.4018/978-1-5225-1941-6.ch001

Levy, C. L., & Elias, N. I. (2017). SOHO Users' Perceptions of Reliability and Continuity of Cloud-Based Services. In M. Moore (Ed.), *Cybersecurity Breaches and Issues Surrounding Online Threat Protection* (pp. 248–287). Hershey, PA: IGI Global. doi:10.4018/978-1-5225-1941-6.ch011

Loganathan, S. (2018). A Step-by-Step Procedural Methodology for Improving an Organization's IT Risk Management System. In M. Gupta, R. Sharman, J. Walp, & P. Mulgund (Eds.), *Information Technology Risk Management and Compliance in Modern Organizations* (pp. 21–47). Hershey, PA: IGI Global. doi:10.4018/978-1-5225-2604-9.ch002

Mahmood, Z. (2016). Cloud Computing Technologies for Open Connected Government. In Z. Mahmood (Ed.), *Cloud Computing Technologies for Connected Government* (pp. 1–14). Hershey, PA: IGI Global. doi:10.4018/978-1-4666-8629-8.ch001

Maiti, P., Addya, S. K., Sahoo, B., & Turuk, A. K. (2017). Energy Efficient Wireless Body Area Network (WBAN). In N. Ray & A. Turuk (Eds.), *Handbook of Research on Advanced Wireless Sensor Network Applications, Protocols, and Architectures* (pp. 413–432). Hershey, PA: IGI Global. doi:10.4018/978-1-5225-0486-3.ch017

Majeed, H., & Erum, F. (2016). Exploiting Semantics to Improve Classification of Text Corpus. In R. Kannan, R. Rasool, H. Jin, & S. Balasundaram (Eds.), *Managing and Processing Big Data in Cloud Computing* (pp. 23–36). Hershey, PA: IGI Global. doi:10.4018/978-1-4666-9767-6.ch002

Manohari, P. K., & Ray, N. K. (2017). A Comprehensive Study of Security in Cloud Computing. In N. Ray & A. Turuk (Eds.), *Handbook of Research on Advanced Wireless Sensor Network Applications, Protocols, and Architectures* (pp. 386–412). Hershey, PA: IGI Global. doi:10.4018/978-1-5225-0486-3.ch016

Manzoor, A. (2016). Cloud Computing Applications in the Public Sector. In Z. Mahmood (Ed.), *Cloud Computing Technologies for Connected Government* (pp. 215–246). Hershey, PA: IGI Global. doi:10.4018/978-1-4666-8629-8.ch009

Marzantowicz, K., & Paciorkowski, Ł. (2017). Community Cloud: Closing the Gap between Public and Private. In J. Chen, Y. Zhang, & R. Gottschalk (Eds.), *Handbook of Research on End-to-End Cloud Computing Architecture Design* (pp. 39–55). Hershey, PA: IGI Global. doi:10.4018/978-1-5225-0759-8.ch003

Meghanathan, N. (2017). Impact of the Structure of the Data Gathering Trees on Node Lifetime and Network Lifetime in Wireless Sensor Networks. In N. Ray & A. Turuk (Eds.), *Handbook of Research on Advanced Wireless Sensor Network Applications, Protocols, and Architectures* (pp. 184–196). Hershey, PA: IGI Global. doi:10.4018/978-1-5225-0486-3.ch007

Memishi, B., Ibrahim, S., Perez, M. S., & Antoniu, G. (2016). On the Dynamic Shifting of the MapReduce Timeout. In R. Kannan, R. Rasool, H. Jin, & S. Balasundaram (Eds.), *Managing and Processing Big Data in Cloud Computing* (pp. 1–22). Hershey, PA: IGI Global. doi:10.4018/978-1-4666-9767-6.ch001

Meralto, C., Moura, J., & Marinheiro, R. (2017). Wireless Mesh Sensor Networks with Mobile Devices: A Comprehensive Review. In N. Ray & A. Turuk (Eds.), *Handbook of Research on Advanced Wireless Sensor Network Applications, Protocols, and Architectures* (pp. 129–155). Hershey, PA: IGI Global. doi:10.4018/978-1-5225-0486-3.ch005

Minto-Coy, I. D., & Henlin, M. G. (2017). The Development of Cybersecurity Policy and Legislative Landscape in Latin America and Caribbean States. In M. Moore (Ed.), *Cybersecurity Breaches and Issues Surrounding Online Threat Protection* (pp. 24–53). Hershey, PA: IGI Global. doi:10.4018/978-1-5225-1941-6.ch002

Mishra, A. K. (2017). Security Threats in Wireless Sensor Networks. In N. Ray & A. Turuk (Eds.), *Handbook of Research on Advanced Wireless Sensor Network Applications, Protocols, and Architectures* (pp. 307–325). Hershey, PA: IGI Global. doi:10.4018/978-1-5225-0486-3.ch012

Mishra, S., Mohapatra, S. K., Mishra, B. K., & Sahoo, S. (2018). Analysis of Mobile Cloud Computing: Architecture, Applications, Challenges, and Future Perspectives. In P. Karthikeyan & M. Thangavel (Eds.), *Applications of Security, Mobile, Analytic, and Cloud (SMAC) Technologies for Effective Information Processing and Management* (pp. 81–104). Hershey, PA: IGI Global. doi:10.4018/978-1-5225-4044-1.ch005

Mohammed, D., Omar, M., & Nguyen, V. (2017). Enhancing Cyber Security for Financial Industry through Compliance and Regulatory Standards. In M. Dawson, M. Eltayeb, & M. Omar (Eds.), *Security Solutions for Hyperconnectivity and the Internet of Things* (pp. 113–129). Hershey, PA: IGI Global. doi:10.4018/978-1-5225-0741-3.ch005

Mohammed, L. A. (2017). Managing Risk in Cloud Computing. In K. Munir (Ed.), *Security Management in Mobile Cloud Computing* (pp. 73–91). Hershey, PA: IGI Global. doi:10.4018/978-1-5225-0602-7.ch004

Mohan, K., Palanisamy, P. B., Kanagachidambaresan, G., Rajesh, S., & Narendran, S. (2018). Role of Security Mechanisms in the Building Blocks of the Cloud Infrastructure. In P. Karthikeyan & M. Thangavel (Eds.), *Applications of Security, Mobile, Analytic, and Cloud (SMAC) Technologies for Effective Information Processing and Management* (pp. 1–23). Hershey, PA: IGI Global. doi:10.4018/978-1-5225-4044-1.ch001

Mohanty, J. P., & Mandal, C. (2017). Connected Dominating Set in Wireless Sensor Network. In N. Ray & A. Turuk (Eds.), *Handbook of Research on Advanced Wireless Sensor Network Applications, Protocols, and Architectures* (pp. 62–85). Hershey, PA: IGI Global. doi:10.4018/978-1-5225-0486-3.ch003

Mohanty, R. P., Turuk, A. K., & Sahoo, B. (2016). Designing of High Performance Multicore Processor with Improved Cache Configuration and Interconnect. In G. Deka, G. Siddesh, K. Srinivasa, & L. Patnaik (Eds.), *Emerging Research Surrounding Power Consumption and Performance Issues in Utility Computing* (pp. 204–219). Hershey, PA: IGI Global. doi:10.4018/978-1-4666-8853-7.ch009

Mohanty, S., Patra, P. K., & Mohapatra, S. (2016). Dynamic Task Assignment with Load Balancing in Cloud Platform. In G. Deka, G. Siddesh, K. Srinivasa, & L. Patnaik (Eds.), *Emerging Research Surrounding Power Consumption and Performance Issues in Utility Computing* (pp. 363–385). Hershey, PA: IGI Global. doi:10.4018/978-1-4666-8853-7.ch018

Mohanty, S., & Patra, S. K. (2017). Performance Evaluation of Quality of Service in IEEE 802.15.4-Based Wireless Sensor Networks. In N. Ray & A. Turuk (Eds.), *Handbook of Research on Advanced Wireless Sensor Network Applications, Protocols, and Architectures* (pp. 213–248). Hershey, PA: IGI Global. doi:10.4018/978-1-5225-0486-3.ch009

Mosthaf, J., & Wagner, H. (2016). The Architect's Role in Business-IT Alignment. *International Journal of IT/Business Alignment and Governance*, 7(1), 36–49. doi:10.4018/IJITBAG.2016010103

Mukherjee, S., Geethapriya, R., & Surianarayanan, S. (2016). A Cloud-Based Framework for Connected Governance. In Z. Mahmood (Ed.), *Cloud Computing Technologies for Connected Government* (pp. 94–123). Hershey, PA: IGI Global. doi:10.4018/978-1-4666-8629-8.ch005

Munir, K. (2017). Security Model for Mobile Cloud Database as a Service (DBaaS). In K. Munir (Ed.), *Security Management in Mobile Cloud Computing* (pp. 169–180). Hershey, PA: IGI Global. doi:10.4018/978-1-5225-0602-7.ch008

Mwirigi, G. B., Zo, H., Rho, J. J., & Park, M. J. (2017). An Empirical Investigation of M-Government Acceptance in Developing Countries: A Case of Kenya. In S. Zoughbi (Ed.), *Securing Government Information and Data in Developing Countries* (pp. 62–89). Hershey, PA: IGI Global. doi:10.4018/978-1-5225-1703-0.ch004

Nanda, A., Popat, P., & Vimalkumar, D. (2018). Navigating Through Choppy Waters of PCI DSS Compliance. In M. Gupta, R. Sharman, J. Walp, & P. Mulgund (Eds.), *Information Technology Risk Management and Compliance in Modern Organizations* (pp. 99–140). Hershey, PA: IGI Global. doi:10.4018/978-1-5225-2604-9.ch005

Narayanapppa, M. T., Channabasamma, A., & Hegadi, R. S. (2016). Need of Hadoop and Map Reduce for Processing and Managing Big Data. In R. Kannan, R. Rasool, H. Jin, & S. Balasundaram (Eds.), *Managing and Processing Big Data in Cloud Computing* (pp. 132–144). Hershey, PA: IGI Global. doi:10.4018/978-1-4666-9767-6.ch009

Narayanapppa, M. T., Kumar, T. P., & Hegadi, R. S. (2016). Essentiality of Machine Learning Algorithms for Big Data Computation. In R. Kannan, R. Rasool, H. Jin, & S. Balasundaram (Eds.), *Managing and Processing Big Data in Cloud Computing* (pp. 156–167). Hershey, PA: IGI Global. doi:10.4018/978-1-4666-9767-6.ch011

Nayak, P. (2017). Internet of Things Services, Applications, Issues, and Challenges. In N. Ray & A. Turuk (Eds.), *Handbook of Research on Advanced Wireless Sensor Network Applications, Protocols, and Architectures* (pp. 353–368). Hershey, PA: IGI Global. doi:10.4018/978-1-5225-0486-3.ch014

Nobles, C. (2017). Cyber Threats in Civil Aviation. In M. Dawson, M. Eltayeb, & M. Omar (Eds.), *Security Solutions for Hyperconnectivity and the Internet of Things* (pp. 272–301). Hershey, PA: IGI Global. doi:10.4018/978-1-5225-0741-3.ch011

Omar, M., Ahmad, K., & Rizvi, M. (2016). Content Based Image Retrieval System. In G. Deka, G. Siddesh, K. Srinivasa, & L. Patnaik (Eds.), *Emerging Research Surrounding Power Consumption and Performance Issues in Utility Computing* (pp. 345–362). Hershey, PA: IGI Global. doi:10.4018/978-1-4666-8853-7.ch017

Panda, S. (2017). Security Issues and Challenges in Internet of Things. In N. Ray & A. Turuk (Eds.), *Handbook of Research on Advanced Wireless Sensor Network Applications, Protocols, and Architectures* (pp. 369–385). Hershey, PA: IGI Global. doi:10.4018/978-1-5225-0486-3.ch015

Pang, C. (2016). An Agile Architecture for a Legacy Enterprise IT System. *International Journal of Organizational and Collective Intelligence*, 6(4), 65–97. doi:10.4018/IJOCI.2016100104

Parkavi, R., Priyanka, C., Sujitha, S., & Sheik Abdullah, A. (2018). Mobile Cloud Computing: Applications Perspective. In P. Karthikeyan & M. Thangavel (Eds.), *Applications of Security, Mobile, Analytic, and Cloud (SMAC) Technologies for Effective Information Processing and Management* (pp. 105–123). Hershey, PA: IGI Global. doi:10.4018/978-1-5225-4044-1.ch006

Pattabiraman, A., Srinivasan, S., Swaminathan, K., & Gupta, M. (2018). Fortifying Corporate Human Wall: A Literature Review of Security Awareness and Training. In M. Gupta, R. Sharman, J. Walp, & P. Mulgund (Eds.), *Information Technology Risk Management and Compliance in Modern Organizations* (pp. 142–175). Hershey, PA: IGI Global. doi:10.4018/978-1-5225-2604-9.ch006

Piraghaj, S. F., Dastjerdi, A. V., Calheiros, R. N., & Buyya, R. (2017). A Survey and Taxonomy of Energy Efficient Resource Management Techniques in Platform as a Service Cloud. In J. Chen, Y. Zhang, & R. Gottschalk (Eds.), *Handbook of Research on End-to-End Cloud Computing Architecture Design* (pp. 410–454). Hershey, PA: IGI Global. doi:10.4018/978-1-5225-0759-8.ch017

Pop, D., Echeverria, A., Petcu, D., & Conesa, G. (2016). Enabling Open and Collaborative Public Service Advertising through Cloud Technologies. In Z. Mahmood (Ed.), *Cloud Computing Technologies for Connected Government* (pp. 269–290). Hershey, PA: IGI Global. doi:10.4018/978-1-4666-8629-8.ch011

Posea, I., Ion, M., Pop, F., Popescu, D., & Popescu, N. (2016). E-Vote: A Cloud-Based Electronic Voting System for Large-Scale Election. In Z. Mahmood (Ed.), *Cloud Computing Technologies for Connected Government* (pp. 188–213). Hershey, PA: IGI Global. doi:10.4018/978-1-4666-8629-8.ch008

Pramanik, P. K., Pal, S., Brahmachari, A., & Choudhury, P. (2018). Processing IoT Data: From Cloud to Fog—It's Time to Be Down to Earth. In P. Karthikeyan & M. Thangavel (Eds.), *Applications of Security, Mobile, Analytic, and Cloud (SMAC) Technologies for Effective Information Processing and Management* (pp. 124–148). Hershey, PA: IGI Global. doi:10.4018/978-1-5225-4044-1.ch007

Prusty, A. R., Sethi, S., & Nayak, A. K. (2017). Energy Aware Optimized Routing Protocols for Wireless Ad Hoc Sensor Network. In N. Ray & A. Turuk (Eds.), *Handbook of Research on Advanced Wireless Sensor Network Applications, Protocols, and Architectures* (pp. 156–183). Hershey, PA: IGI Global. doi:10.4018/978-1-5225-0486-3.ch006

Related Readings

Pudumalar, S., Suriya, K. S., & Rohini, K. (2018). Data Classification and Prediction. In P. Karthikeyan & M. Thangavel (Eds.), *Applications of Security, Mobile, Analytic, and Cloud (SMAC) Technologies for Effective Information Processing and Management* (pp. 149–173). Hershey, PA: IGI Global. doi:10.4018/978-1-5225-4044-1.ch008

Qamar, M., Malik, M., Batool, S., Mehmood, S., Malik, A. W., & Rahman, A. (2016). Centralized to Decentralized Social Networks: Factors that Matter. In R. Kannan, R. Rasool, H. Jin, & S. Balasundaram (Eds.), *Managing and Processing Big Data in Cloud Computing* (pp. 37–54). Hershey, PA: IGI Global. doi:10.4018/978-1-4666-9767-6.ch003

Raj, P. (2016). Significance of Clouds for Connected Governments: The Government Clouds in India. In Z. Mahmood (Ed.), *Cloud Computing Technologies for Connected Government* (pp. 15–38). Hershey, PA: IGI Global. doi:10.4018/978-1-4666-8629-8.ch002

Richardson, L., & Mukherjea, S. (2017). Enterprise Mobility Reference Architecture: Mobility Services Overview. In J. Chen, Y. Zhang, & R. Gottschalk (Eds.), *Handbook of Research on End-to-End Cloud Computing Architecture Design* (pp. 1–14). Hershey, PA: IGI Global. doi:10.4018/978-1-5225-0759-8.ch001

Rout, S., Turuk, A. K., & Sahoo, B. (2017). Techniques to Enhance the Lifetime of MANET. In N. Ray & A. Turuk (Eds.), *Handbook of Research on Advanced Wireless Sensor Network Applications, Protocols, and Architectures* (pp. 278–306). Hershey, PA: IGI Global. doi:10.4018/978-1-5225-0486-3.ch011

Roy, S., Ahuja, S. P., Harish, P. D., & Talluri, S. R. (2018). Energy Optimization in Cryptographic Protocols for the Cloud. In P. Karthikeyan & M. Thangavel (Eds.), *Applications of Security, Mobile, Analytic, and Cloud (SMAC) Technologies for Effective Information Processing and Management* (pp. 24–48). Hershey, PA: IGI Global. doi:10.4018/978-1-5225-4044-1.ch002

S., S., & R., P. (2017). Cybercrime Investigation. In M. Moore (Ed.), *Cybersecurity Breaches and Issues Surrounding Online Threat Protection* (pp. 96-120). Hershey, PA: IGI Global. doi:10.4018/978-1-5225-1941-6.ch005

S., T., & Pahwa, B. (2017). Empowering IT with Green Computing. In N. Ray, & A. Turuk (Eds.), *Handbook of Research on Advanced Wireless Sensor Network Applications, Protocols, and Architectures* (pp. 433-450). Hershey, PA: IGI Global. doi:10.4018/978-1-5225-0486-3.ch018

Sethi, S., & Sahoo, R. K. (2017). Design of WSN in Real Time Application of Health Monitoring System. In N. Ray & A. Turuk (Eds.), *Handbook of Research on Advanced Wireless Sensor Network Applications, Protocols, and Architectures* (pp. 197–212). Hershey, PA: IGI Global. doi:10.4018/978-1-5225-0486-3.ch008

Shalan, M. A. (2017). Considering Middle Circles in Mobile Cloud Computing: Ethics and Risk Governance. In K. Munir (Ed.), *Security Management in Mobile Cloud Computing* (pp. 43–72). Hershey, PA: IGI Global. doi:10.4018/978-1-5225-0602-7.ch003

Shalan, M. A. (2017). Risk and Governance Considerations in Cloud Era. In J. Chen, Y. Zhang, & R. Gottschalk (Eds.), *Handbook of Research on End-to-End Cloud Computing Architecture Design* (pp. 376–409). Hershey, PA: IGI Global. doi:10.4018/978-1-5225-0759-8.ch016

Shamsolmoali, P., Zareapoor, M., & Alam, M. (2017). Multi-Aspect DDOS Detection System for Securing Cloud Network. In J. Chen, Y. Zhang, & R. Gottschalk (Eds.), *Handbook of Research on End-to-End Cloud Computing Architecture Design* (pp. 222–252). Hershey, PA: IGI Global. doi:10.4018/978-1-5225-0759-8.ch010

Shen, L., Chen, I., & Su, A. (2017). Cybersecurity and Data Breaches at Schools. In M. Moore (Ed.), *Cybersecurity Breaches and Issues Surrounding Online Threat Protection* (pp. 144–174). Hershey, PA: IGI Global. doi:10.4018/978-1-5225-1941-6.ch007

Silva, N., Ferreira, F., Sousa, P., & Mira da Silva, M. (2016). Automating the Migration of Enterprise Architecture Models. *International Journal of Information System Modeling and Design*, 7(2), 72–90. doi:10.4018/IJISMD.2016040104

Singh, B., & K.S., J. (2017). Security Management in Mobile Cloud Computing: Security and Privacy Issues and Solutions in Mobile Cloud Computing. In K. Munir (Ed.), *Security Management in Mobile Cloud Computing* (pp. 148-168). Hershey, PA: IGI Global. doi:10.4018/978-1-5225-0602-7.ch007

Singh, N., Mittal, T., & Gupta, M. (2018). A Tale of Policies and Breaches: Analytical Approach to Construct Social Media Policy. In M. Gupta, R. Sharman, J. Walp, & P. Mulgund (Eds.), *Information Technology Risk Management and Compliance in Modern Organizations* (pp. 176–212). Hershey, PA: IGI Global. doi:10.4018/978-1-5225-2604-9.ch007

Singh, S., & Gond, S. (2016). Green Computing and Its Impact. In G. Deka, G. Siddesh, K. Srinivasa, & L. Patnaik (Eds.), *Emerging Research Surrounding Power Consumption and Performance Issues in Utility Computing* (pp. 69–83). Hershey, PA: IGI Global. doi:10.4018/978-1-4666-8853-7.ch004

Sivagurunathan, S., & Swasthimathi, L. S. (2016). Cloud Computing Applications in Education through E-Governance: An Indian Perspective. In Z. Mahmood (Ed.), *Cloud Computing Technologies for Connected Government* (pp. 247–268). Hershey, PA: IGI Global. doi:10.4018/978-1-4666-8629-8.ch010

Soni, P. (2018). Implications of HIPAA and Subsequent Regulations on Information Technology. In M. Gupta, R. Sharman, J. Walp, & P. Mulgund (Eds.), *Information Technology Risk Management and Compliance in Modern Organizations* (pp. 71–98). Hershey, PA: IGI Global. doi:10.4018/978-1-5225-2604-9.ch004

Srinivasa, K. G., Hegde, G., Sideesh, G. M., & Hiriyannaiah, S. (2016). A Viability Analysis of an Economical Private Cloud Storage Solution Powered by Raspberry Pi in the NSA Era: A Survey and Analysis of Cost and Security. In G. Deka, G. Siddesh, K. Srinivasa, & L. Patnaik (Eds.), *Emerging Research Surrounding Power Consumption and Performance Issues in Utility Computing* (pp. 220–232). Hershey, PA: IGI Global. doi:10.4018/978-1-4666-8853-7.ch010

Srinivasa, K. G., Siddesh, G. M., Hiriyannaiah, S., Mishra, K., Prajeeth, C. S., & Talha, A. M. (2016). GPU Implementation of Friend Recommendation System using CUDA for Social Networking Services. In G. Deka, G. Siddesh, K. Srinivasa, & L. Patnaik (Eds.), *Emerging Research Surrounding Power Consumption and Performance Issues in Utility Computing* (pp. 304–319). Hershey, PA: IGI Global. doi:10.4018/978-1-4666-8853-7.ch015

Suresh, N., & Gupta, M. (2018). Impact of Technology Innovation: A Study on Cloud Risk Mitigation. In M. Gupta, R. Sharman, J. Walp, & P. Mulgund (Eds.), *Information Technology Risk Management and Compliance in Modern Organizations* (pp. 229–267). Hershey, PA: IGI Global. doi:10.4018/978-1-5225-2604-9.ch009

Susanto, H., & Almunawar, M. N. (2016). Security and Privacy Issues in Cloud-Based E-Government. In Z. Mahmood (Ed.), *Cloud Computing Technologies for Connected Government* (pp. 292–321). Hershey, PA: IGI Global. doi:10.4018/978-1-4666-8629-8.ch012

Suthakar, K. I., & Devi, M. K. (2016). Resource Scheduling for Big Data on Cloud: Scheduling Resources. In R. Kannan, R. Rasool, H. Jin, & S. Balasundaram (Eds.), *Managing and Processing Big Data in Cloud Computing* (pp. 185–205). Hershey, PA: IGI Global. doi:10.4018/978-1-4666-9767-6.ch013

Swarnkar, M., & Bhadoria, R. S. (2016). Security Aspects in Utility Computing. In G. Deka, G. Siddesh, K. Srinivasa, & L. Patnaik (Eds.), *Emerging Research Surrounding Power Consumption and Performance Issues in Utility Computing* (pp. 262–275). Hershey, PA: IGI Global. doi:10.4018/978-1-4666-8853-7.ch012

Tank, D. M. (2017). Security and Privacy Issues, Solutions, and Tools for MCC. In K. Munir (Ed.), *Security Management in Mobile Cloud Computing* (pp. 121–147). Hershey, PA: IGI Global. doi:10.4018/978-1-5225-0602-7.ch006

Thio, C., & Cook, J. (2017). Workload Migration to Cloud. In J. Chen, Y. Zhang, & R. Gottschalk (Eds.), *Handbook of Research on End-to-End Cloud Computing Architecture Design* (pp. 279–298). Hershey, PA: IGI Global. doi:10.4018/978-1-5225-0759-8.ch012

Thota, C., Manogaran, G., Lopez, D., & Vijayakumar, V. (2017). Big Data Security Framework for Distributed Cloud Data Centers. In M. Moore (Ed.), *Cybersecurity Breaches and Issues Surrounding Online Threat Protection* (pp. 288–310). Hershey, PA: IGI Global. doi:10.4018/978-1-5225-1941-6.ch012

Umair, S., Muneer, U., Zahoor, M. N., & Malik, A. W. (2016). Mobile Cloud Computing Future Trends and Opportunities. In R. Kannan, R. Rasool, H. Jin, & S. Balasundaram (Eds.), *Managing and Processing Big Data in Cloud Computing* (pp. 105–120). Hershey, PA: IGI Global. doi:10.4018/978-1-4666-9767-6.ch007

Venkateswaran, S. (2017). Industrial Patterns on Cloud. In J. Chen, Y. Zhang, & R. Gottschalk (Eds.), *Handbook of Research on End-to-End Cloud Computing Architecture Design* (pp. 73–103). Hershey, PA: IGI Global. doi:10.4018/978-1-5225-0759-8.ch005

Wolfe, M. (2017). Establishing Governance for Hybrid Cloud and the Internet of Things. In J. Chen, Y. Zhang, & R. Gottschalk (Eds.), *Handbook of Research on End-to-End Cloud Computing Architecture Design* (pp. 300–325). Hershey, PA: IGI Global. doi:10.4018/978-1-5225-0759-8.ch013

Yahaya, M. O. (2017). On the Role of Game Theory in Modelling Incentives and Interactions in Mobile Distributed Systems. In K. Munir (Ed.), *Security Management in Mobile Cloud Computing* (pp. 92–120). Hershey, PA: IGI Global. doi:10.4018/978-1-5225-0602-7.ch005

Zhang, W., Qi, Q., & Deng, J. (2017). Building Intelligent Transportation Cloud Data Center Based on SOA. *International Journal of Ambient Computing and Intelligence*, 8(2), 1–11. doi:10.4018/IJACI.2017040101

Zolotow, C., Graf, F., Pfitzmann, B., Huber, R., Schlatter, M., Schrøder-Hansen, C., & Hunt, A. (2017). Transition and Transformation into a Cloud Environment. In J. Chen, Y. Zhang, & R. Gottschalk (Eds.), *Handbook of Research on End-to-End Cloud Computing Architecture Design* (pp. 254–278). Hershey, PA: IGI Global. doi:10.4018/978-1-5225-0759-8.ch011

Related Readings

Zoughbi, S. (2017). Major Issues Affecting Government Data and Information in Developing Countries. In S. Zoughbi (Ed.), *Securing Government Information and Data in Developing Countries* (pp. 115–126). Hershey, PA: IGI Global. doi:10.4018/978-1-5225-1703-0.ch007

Zoughbi, S. (2017). Major Technology Trends Affecting Government Data in Developing Countries. In S. Zoughbi (Ed.), *Securing Government Information and Data in Developing Countries* (pp. 127–135). Hershey, PA: IGI Global. doi:10.4018/978-1-5225-1703-0.ch008

Index

Ensure Quality Research is Introduced to the Academic Community

Become an IGI Global Reviewer for Authored Book Projects

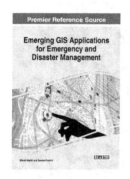

The overall success of an authored book project is dependent on quality and timely reviews.

In this competitive age of scholarly publishing, constructive and timely feedback significantly expedites the turnaround time of manuscripts from submission to acceptance, allowing the publication and discovery of forward-thinking research at a much more expeditious rate. Several IGI Global authored book projects are currently seeking highly qualified experts in the field to fill vacancies on their respective editorial review boards:

Applications may be sent to:
development@igi-global.com

Applicants must have a doctorate (or an equivalent degree) as well as publishing and reviewing experience. Reviewers are asked to write reviews in a timely, collegial, and constructive manner. All reviewers will begin their role on an ad-hoc basis for a period of one year, and upon successful completion of this term can be considered for full editorial review board status, with the potential for a subsequent promotion to Associate Editor.

If you have a colleague that may be interested in this opportunity, we encourage you to share this information with them.

Printed in the United States
By Bookmasters